RAISING JESS

A STORY OF HOPE

Photo by Brian Smistek

Vickie Rubin

PAGE PUBLISHING, INC.
Conneaut Lake, PA

First originally published by Page Publishing 2021

ISBN 978-1-6624-0741-3 (pbk)
ISBN 978-1-6624-6052-4 (hc)
ISBN 978-1-6624-0742-0 (digital)

Printed in the United States of America

To Jessica, who changed my life.

To Mom, who gave me life and always said, "You should write a book." I wish you were here to see it come true.

CONTENTS

Life's under no obligation to give us what we expect.

—Margaret Mitchell

I thought I would have to teach my child about the world. It turns out, I have to teach the world about my child.

—Source Unknown

CHAPTER 1

Our Esther Bunny

On April 11, 1982, Easter Sunday, I was twenty-four years old and had the chicken pox. And I was about to deliver my first child. For a week I had complained to my doctor about a rash, and for a week he had said, "The baby is settling. Do not worry;" or, "Just put some lotion on. It must be dry skin." I was naïve, pregnant, unaware, and truly wanted to believe it was nothing.

And then my water broke. We arrived at the local hospital, and as I told a few doctors about my rash, each dismissed it as unimportant, until finally an astute nurse (probably an experienced mother) said to me that my rash looked like chicken pox. My mind went into overdrive, racing with anxious thoughts. How could this be? I was in labor and I was twenty-four years old. Didn't I already have all the childhood diseases? They called in other doctors to confirm the suspected diagnosis, and since nobody was sure, a physician ordered a biopsy of my rash to confirm that I indeed had chicken pox. I clearly remember a labor pain and a scalpel removing a pox happening simultaneously. Welcome to motherhood.

Once the chicken pox diagnosis was confirmed, the local hospital had trouble dealing with the ridiculous news. My husband, Mitch, had the misfortune of a new resident telling him that it was unlikely the baby and I would survive the birth and delivery. He actually said that. Perhaps in the late 1970s and early '80s, medical schools didn't include the class on how to talk to patients and families. Perhaps the resident was so overwhelmed with chicken pox, labor, and a frantic mom-to-be that he just blurted out what he was thinking rather than considering what he should say. I wonder if he is still in medicine and if he ever thinks of this incident from Easter Sunday in 1982.

Mitch contacted my parents, who were in Florida and were unable to fly to Buffalo on such short notice on Easter Sunday. They would have to wait until Monday. My in-laws were at the hospital with us, praying for a positive outcome.

The attending doctor decided that I should be moved to Buffalo Children's Hospital (now called Oishei Children's Hospital of Buffalo, Kaleida Health). One would assume that I would be transported by ambulance, but Mitch drove the twenty-five-minute route with me laboring beside him. My labor was at the beginning stages, and since it was my first child, I believe the doctors at the first hospital thought I was not in danger of giving birth on the highway. In today's litigious world, I think they would not have taken that chance.

Meanwhile, my father-in-law was sent on a mission to get what we were told was the last vial of the varicella-zoster vaccine (for chicken pox) to administer to the baby as soon as she was born. The problem was that on Easter, the only pharmacy that had this drug was Roswell Park Cancer Hospital, and they were closing within the hour. We were told it was the only place to get it in the city. Again, it's hard to believe that in 1982 the hospital would send my father-in-law to pick up crucial medication. What if something happened to his car, or he dropped the medication and it shattered, or he encountered any number of random acts of delay? Buffalo was not a rural town in the 1980s, but the way this day was unfolding, one would think we lived in Mayberry (a small town in a 1960s sitcom, for you millennials).

Mitch and I arrived safely at Buffalo Children's Hospital, and to our surprise, the medical staff was not alarmed about my circumstances. They admitted me into an isolation room so as not to spread chicken pox in the labor and delivery unit or among fellow newborns. My father-in-law was able to get the medicine while I labored for eight more uncomfortable hours at the hospital.

Jessica was born on April 11, 1982, at 8:15 p.m. and our friend Jackie promptly dubbed her our Esther Bunny, her nickname for a Jewish baby girl born on Easter. Jessica did not have chicken pox and was immediately administered the drug my father-in-law had fetched from the cancer hospital. Jess was taken to the neonatal intensive care unit (NICU) for monitoring, and since this was 1982, I was unable to see my firstborn child. There was no cell phone, FaceTime, texting, Facebook, Instagram—nothing. The 1982 version of instant photos was a Polaroid camera. Mitch bought a camera and showered me with photos of our newborn; however, I was desperate to hold Jessica in person. My mom-hormones were screaming to hold my newborn while the physicians reminded me that I was still contagious.

I was released from the hospital within thirty-six hours, but was unable to see our baby or bring her home until a pediatrician in the community declared that I was chicken pox free. In hindsight, I question why I wasn't referred to an infectious disease specialist at the hospital or perhaps to a dermatologist, as it was skin related. Fortunately, I found a pediatrician who cleared me and sent me on my way home to motherhood.

Jessica weighed less than five pounds when she was born, although she was not delivered early. In retrospect, it was obvious that Jess had unusual facial features and other anomalies, but as first-time parents, we were somewhat clueless, and the doctors did not say anything to us. We had a baby nurse who had been in the profession for over thirty years and who assisted us for the first month. She said Jess was the tiniest baby she had cared for, but she didn't remark on any other differences.

In Long Island, New York where I was raised, baby nurses were commonplace when a mom came home with her newborn. My mom was not a hands-on parent, but she was extremely generous with funds. Mom insisted that I have a baby nurse for the first month and that she would pay. I didn't have to think twice about that offer; however, this was not a common practice in the suburbs of Buffalo where we lived. I searched high and low for a baby nurse and was repeatedly asked if I had a disability or some problem that prevented me from caring for my newborn. I replied that unless being spoiled by my parents is a disability, I was okay. We selected a nurse after an out-of-town friend referred her to us.

As the months passed, the pediatrician continued to assure us that Jess was developing normally, and I continued to question all her delays. Interestingly, in reexamination, an inexperienced mom like me knew more about her child than an experienced physician.

I recently came across a letter written by my father that applauds Mitch's and my ability to manage the difficult birth and circumstances. He concluded in his letter that this was a brief hiccup of a start and that he looked forward to seeing Jessica develop into a wonderful daughter whom we could be proud of as he was of me. Jessica has developed into a wonderful daughter and we have much pride, but her story is very different from mine.

Little did we know that chicken pox was the least of our worries.

With great joy and love
we announce the birth
of our daughter

Jessica Layne
on Sunday, April 11, 1982
8:15 p.m.

Vickie and Mitchel Rubin

Birth announcement.

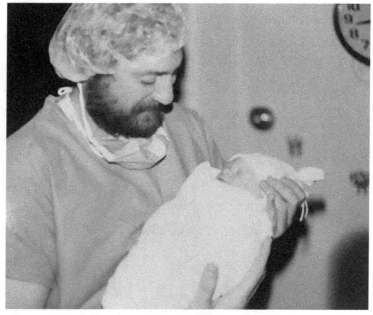

Jess and Mitch.

Vickie and Jess.

Vickie, Mitch, Jessica, and Tracey, 1982.

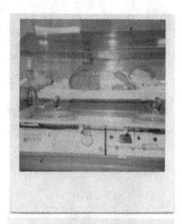

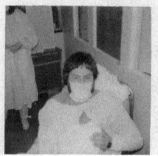

Jess in an incubator at Children's Hospital of
Buffalo, Neonatal Intensive Care Unit, April 1982.

Jessica, 1982

Professional family photo, including Tracey our dog.

Hypochondria, OCD, or Mother's Intuition?

I have been called a hypochondriac, told I have obsessive-compulsive disorder (OCD), and accused of incessant worrying. So it was not unexpected that I would take Jess to the pediatrician—a lot.

When Jess was two months old and it felt safe to bring my tiny princess around other children, I started to meet other babies and their moms. The difference in development between their infants and Jess was becoming evident, at least to me.

When Jess was born, I thoroughly researched pediatricians so that she would have the best care—at any rate that was my intention. I was keen on doing this right, but as it turned out, our first pediatrician did not have the experience that I needed. Even with all my diligent research, Dr. Dismissal (not his real name) refused to agree that Jessica needed a developmental evaluation, although the signs were clearly there. Her head size was in the range of microcephaly—abnormal smallness of the head circumference, usually associated with an intellectual disability. The data was clear.

My Journal Entries:

Wednesday, June 16, 1982, 3:30
— How can we make Jess gain more weight
— Jerky head movement and banging
— Smile? Should she be smiling (doctor suggested a hearing test)
— Doesn't seem to respond to me (Doctor again suggested hearing test)

July 1, 1982, 2:45 pm
— Is Jess growing at a normal pace for her size? [in comparison to her small birth weight]
— Is her head growing normally

September 8, 1992
- — Not lifting her head or flipping over
- — Is there any exercises I can do to help her lift her head or start grasping objects

Why didn't he know the signs? How I wish that I had a doctor who understood the various concerns we had about our daughter. There were other naysayers besides our pediatrician such as in-laws and friends, and even my husband wasn't completely on my ship. It was as if he was on the gangplank but not ready to climb aboard. One memorable comment from the pediatrician during one of our frequent visits was that I should probably seek counseling, since Jess was fine. I guess he was not so dismissive of my own issues.

In retrospect, I probably did need counseling, but that had nothing to do with my concerns for Jess. I remained in this circular pattern for six months: visit pediatrician, fears examined and dismissed, home again with fears building, and back to the pediatrician for another dismissal. It was exhausting.

Many months passed as we continued to make appointments only to be brushed off by the doctor. Unable to convince Dr. Dismissal, I did what every good Long Island Jewish girl does and called my mother. Mom immediately made an appointment with a top pediatric neurologist on October 19, 1982, and I went back to my homeland of Long Island, New York, to search for another opinion. My mother, Jess, and I met with a pediatric neurologist at North Shore Jewish Hospital. It was extremely unnerving to watch all the tests that were given and then waiting, waiting, waiting to hear a result. Did I really want to know?

It was both a heart-wrenching and disturbing experience. Imagine sitting in the office, knowing that something was wrong with your child and watching test after test administered with possible dire results. It was hard to process the information. Even though my intuition told me that Jessica was delayed, hearing the confirmation was another story. One is never really prepared for this type of news.

Finally, the doctor sat my mother and me down and confirmed that Jessica was delayed in every milestone and she had microcephaly (a small head). She was six months old and was already failing every test. Unfortunately, the only test that I had passed was the mother-knows-best test.

I went back to my parents' home that evening, and my mind was a blur. I wasn't sure what this meant for Jessica and our family. How would her life be different, and how would our life be different? Did I really have what it took to do this? I thought about one of my undergraduate teachers at the University of Miami who suggested that I pursue a degree in special education; at the time I was earning a bachelor's in elementary education. My immediate reply was that I wouldn't have the patience for special education. Would that statement come back to haunt me?

Later that evening we took Jessica to our neighbor, Natalie Ginsburg, house. so that she could watch Jess while my parents took me out to dinner. While many families gather around the kitchen table during a crisis, our family gathers around the restaurant table. (My mother was the epitome of the old joke: What are you making for dinner, honey? Reservations.)

As I was walking Jessica to Natalie's house, my mind was whirling, I couldn't really concentrate on a single thought, but I remember feeling dread and grief. This evening was the only time that I would sense this devastation because from that moment on, I went into fix-it mode.

The doctor from Long Island sent me home with instructions to seek another opinion in Buffalo, New York.

We went to the head of Children's Hospital Rehabilitation Center, and this time Mitch was beside me at the appointment. He heard the truth himself and finally joined me on that boat. My husband recalls this day as the worst day of his life, and in fact, as we reminisce about the visit, he still gets choked up. My husband describes a moment during the appointment where he felt like he was looking at the doctor through binoculars, except they were reversed—the doctor appeared miles away.

Mitch wept for forty-five minutes that day, and when he was done, we put on our big-girl and big-boy pants and decided to move forward with love, determination, teamwork, and a bit of naïveté. I have always wished I could have cried at this moment as Mitch did, but I was unable to cry about our circumstances. My instinct was to get moving and fix this—now.

I often try to evaluate my reaction. Was it because I knew there was a problem for so many months that it was a relief to finally have it corroborated by the experts? Was I too shocked to think about the true meaning of this lifelong sentence? Or was I simply accepting our circumstances and moving on toward our alternate path? I don't have the patience for this analysis, so I will select immediate acceptance of our circumstances as my reason for not shedding tears at the time.

The developmental pediatrician in Buffalo thought that Jessica resembled two of his children who had a genetic abnormality called cri du chat stemming from the fifth chromosome. With Jessica's genetic testing and the doctor's insistence, the lab found that Jess had an interstitial deletion or gap (the missing genetic material was in the middle of the short arm) of her fifth chromosome. So, we had what we thought was finally a diagnosis for Jessica. It was an awful diagnosis that we discovered after reading (remember, no Google) reports of the potentially devastating outcomes for some children with cri du chat, and we realized how awful the diagnosis really was. Many do well, but the medical journals featured photos and outcomes that were alarming and depressing. Ultimately it was found that cri du chat was not a correct diagnosis, but we didn't find that out for another ten years.

Looking back on the first six months of battles with Dr. Dismissal, I do see a positive note. Prior to the start of additional doctor appointments and clinicians, we were able to bond with Jess as a typical infant without all the therapies and professionals invading our new family life. I do not believe the delay in services made a difference in Jessica's outcome.

I admit I was a hypochondriac (I can hear my friends and family who are reading this laughing at "was") and I know I still tend to ruminate on many things, but I think in this instance it worked in our favor. We were starting a new journey, not one that we chose, but nevertheless we embraced our daughter and our mission with full hearts and a commitment to finding a cure. Maybe having a touch of OCD could help move the process just a bit quicker.

Jessica on her first birthday, April 11, 1983.

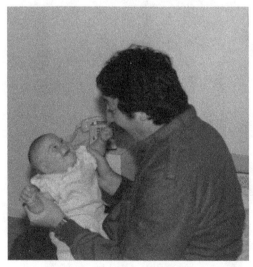

Jess and Mitch, 1982.

Jess and Vickie, 1982-83.

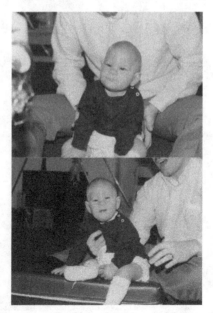

Jessica at Buffalo Children's Hospital
Infant Stimulation Program.

Jess sitting.

Muscle tone is normal. Jessie is beginning to bat at objects.
As of today when an object was placed at her midline she
brought up her hand to grab it. She is extremely vocal,
she has a wide range of sounds although she doesn't say vowels
(ie. CA Da Ah). Jessicas brain scan revealed that her convolutions
were slightly wider than normal, no other abnormalities were
noted.

The following is a chart of Jessie's ht,wt., and head circumference:

DATE	WEIGHT	HEIGHT	HEAD
4-11	4lb. 15oz.	17in.	30cm.
5-13	5lb. 8oz.	18in.	
6-16	6lb.7oz	19in.	13 1/8 in.
7-1	7lb.6oz.	20in.	13 4/8 in.
8-2	8lb9oz	20 3/4 in.	13 3/4 in.
9-8	9lb.15oz.	22 1/8 in.	14 1/4 in.
9-28	10lb. 4oz.		
10-19	fontale 1.5 x1.5 cm.		36 3/4 cm.
11-29	12lb.3oz.	23 1/2 in.	14 3/4 in.

At present, Jessie is enrolled in an infant stimulation

Jessica's weight-height-head statistics, 1982.

CHAPTER 3

It Takes a Village

It was 1982, and there were not a lot of therapeutic options available. This was pre-Early Intervention Program,[1] and as parents, we sometimes felt like we had to make change happen ourselves.

---

[1] Early Intervention Program (EIP) for infants and toddlers with disabilities and their families. First created by Congress in 1986 under the Individuals with Disabilities Education Act (IDEA), the EIP is administered by the New York State Department of Health through the Bureau of Early Intervention. In New York State, the Early Intervention Program is established in Article 25 of the Public Health Law and has been in effect since July 1, 1993. To be eligible for services, children must be under three years of age and have a confirmed disability or established developmental delay, as defined by the state, in one or more of the following areas of development: physical, cognitive, communication, social-emotional, and/or adaptive. https://www.health.ny.gov/community/infants_children/early_intervention/

I am not sure how we found out about the Doman-Delacato method of patterning, but I do remember that it was controversial. The medical professionals were not in agreement, and it was also extremely expensive and time-consuming. In my not-so-scientific explanation, patterning was the act of moving Jessica's arms, legs, torso, and other body parts to create new pathways to the brain. The theory was that since Jess had a congenital disability, she did not develop neurologically or physically normal in the womb; therefore, we were going to make new pathways and *voilà*—Jess would be a typically developing toddler. Spoiler alert: it didn't work, but there were some unintentional benefits.

We did not go to the Institutes for the Achievement of Human Potential (IAHP) in Philadelphia, which is the birthplace of patterning. Traditional patterning at home would have encompassed seven days per week of retraining Jessica's neural pathways. Since we weren't completely convinced of this method, we decided to compromise with patterning four days a week and traditional therapy at Children's Hospital of Buffalo two days per week. And we found Gene. Don't get confused by his name. This is a person, not a genetic discovery. Gene was a patterning expert who trained in Philadelphia and spread the word throughout the country. Gene was not cheap; he cost a lot of bucks, and Mitch and I had very few bucks. My parents came to the rescue to pay for Gene and all his extra costs. Grandparents were also grasping to find a remedy, a cure, a sign of hope. (More about the grandparents' journey in the following chapters.) We had a plan and started our path toward our potential cure.

Recently while cleaning out my closet, I found my list of volunteers and journal from that time. We had forty-two men, women, and even some teens, mostly from our temple, who came to our home four days per week for two 2.5-hour shifts each day. One positive outcome of patterning was all the support we received from dedicated assistants. Each person did it because he or she wanted to make a difference and help a baby. Little did they know how much they were also helping me. Four days per week, 2.5 hours twice per day, we were surrounded by caring and loving support, all focused on helping Jessica—our loving village.

I acknowledge that I was a bit focused on fixing Jess during the early years. If one entered our home, they would have marveled over the vestibular stimulus apparatus in her room that was essentially a large hammock-shaped swing where we would push Jess from side to side while she rested comfortably in the cozy cocoon. We also had a long home-made slant board in our living room where I would push on Jessica's hamstring to encourage combat crawling; the volunteers were our cheering section. I questioned this tactic because it was not comfortable for Jess. Imagine someone squeezing your hamstring so that you will inch forward. The activity did produce temporary results. Jess never showed discomfort, and had she grimaced or cried, I would have stopped immediately. Yet this exercise still felt unpleasant to me and Jess.

Our home was filled with poster boards that described every exercise, complete with directions and timing. One of our treasures was a high table that was built in her bedroom by one of our close friends, Joe C. It was a labor of love, and we kept the table many years after we abandoned patterning. Now in 2019, the table is our garage workbench; quality craftsmanship lasts a lifetime.

Journal Notes

December 20, 1982 was our first day of patterning; we started with only one session that day. I took Jess along with my friend Barb and her baby Emily for a stroll in the afternoon after a full morning of patterning. Jess was wrapped in a snuggly baby holder strapped across my chest. While we were walking, I was unable to wake Jess and Barb and I were convinced that tragedy had struck. We quickly brought Jess into a laundromat which we were passing, and I proceeded to remove Jess from all her contraptions. Jess woke up with a glare as if to say, "I'm not even a year old, you put me through a 2.5-hour training session and then you are surprised when I am tired? Geez!" (As an aside— Barb and I still laugh at this 38 years later.

Yes, we laugh—it's the best medicine we have.)

December 22, 1982—Perhaps Jess was more responsive (wishful thinking?).

January 7, 1983—Jess is sick and I am organizing forty-two volunteers and feeling very overwhelmed... I forgot to contact two volunteers and had to call them at 8:00 a.m. to say, "Hey, can you come by in one hour to volunteer?"

My journal states that "I hope they didn't think I was irresponsible." My sixty-year-old self looks back on my twenty-four-year-old self who was juggling so much and still striving to get it all right, and wishes I had been easier on myself.

Examples of some of the exercises are shown at the end of this chapter. I don't want to belabor the point, so I will give a brief overview of our routine here plus more detailed information after this chapter.

Jess would lie on the high table, and with me leading the four other volunteers, we would move Jessica's wrists, legs, and head in a rhythmic pattern as I called out the cues like a coxswain (cool word—it means crew boat caller). We would start with the wrist and ankle exercise, and in unison, we all twisted left, right, pulled out, and pushed in and continued for five minutes. The feather duster activity entailed tickling Jessica's palms and feet to increase her tactile response. And then there was the beloved brushing exercise, not for hair or teeth; we brushed Jessica's palms and feet to increase sensation in her extremities. To this day, Jessica is very responsive to touch, and so I will give patterning two points for that.

Jessica has always been extremely social, and I believe that all the constant interaction with loving patterners may have set her on that path. But as far as walking, crawling, talking, feeding herself, and other skills of daily living, there were no improvements.

Patterning was stressful. I found a to-do list from 1983 that included asking Gene if I could only show words to Jess upside down (I have no idea what that means), which person oversees Jessica's knees during an exercise, sour cream, cheddar cheese, and refried beans. There was some evidence that I was still trying to at least stay on top of dinner.

In hindsight, the amount of pressure put on families by this therapeutic model was unfair. We were told that each day Jessica didn't learn something new was a day that she would become even more delayed since she had to catch up. We were also told that if patterning didn't work, it was most likely our fault. These are heavy weights to carry, and as inexperienced young parents, we felt that we needed to keep moving—and quickly.

I have notes from a conversation with JK, a friend whose son also went through the program. JK was a huge fan of the method. Her schedule was seven days a week, twelve hours per day (can this be true?). My notes from our conversation detailing her schedule indicate those were their daily hours spent on patterning: "JK's child had a lot of improvements, but she quit after three years. JK's reason was genuine; she said, 'too much money and time.'"

One day my husband was watching sports on TV and Jess was sitting on the couch beside him. I entered the room and quickly remarked that we should be stimulating Jess and that she was wasting time just hanging out. My husband looked me in the eye and said that Jess also had to be our baby girl and spend time sitting on the couch with her dad. He was right, and I wish that statement changed my continuous need to fix Jess. I finally found something that convinced me to stop patterning, but that took more than a year: getting pregnant with our second child.

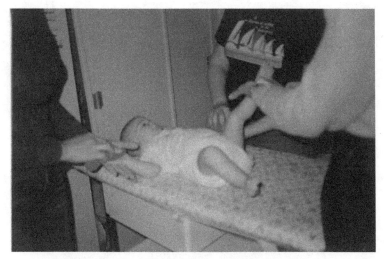

Brushing of hands and feet—patterning exercise.

RE: INITIAL STATEMENT: 9th & 10th December 82 ealuation: Jessica Layne Rubin· Please indicate whether you elect Plan #1 or Plan #2 for future evaluations when you send in your payment for the Inital Evaluation on or before 10 Jan 83. If you elect Plan #1, I will then forwatd to you the necessary addressed envelopes for making monthly payments for future revisits. Thanks, LSL - accts.

PLEASE KEEP THE ORIGINAL COPY FOR YOUR RECORDS AND RETURNED THE CARBON COPY ENCLOSED SO MARKED FOR YOUR ELECTION OF PLAN #1 or #2

CURRENT FEE SCHEDULE

INITIAL - Sensorimotor Neurological Developmental $ 525.00
Evaluation and Instruction in Programmed
Technique Procedures
(TIME ELEMENT: One very lengthy day and
a portion of the night; or portions of
two days)

PLAN #1 - Follow up revisits every 3 to 4 months $ 115.00
(Frequency of revisits determined by the   Monthly
family being seen)

(preferred) $115.00 Monthly Fee Payable Each 30 days
following the Initial Assessment

      If seen every 3 months 4 times
yearly, this averages out when
paid monthly to be $345.00.

      If seen every 4 months 3 times
yearly, this averages out when
paid monthly to be $460.00.

PLAN #2 - Flat Rate Fee follow up revisits
(Frequency of revisits determined by the
family being seen)

(preferred) 3 Month frequency - seen 4 times yearly $ 385.00

            4 Month frequency - seen 3 times yearly $ 495.00

            6 Month frequency - seen 2 times yearly $ 525.00

            Any period exceeding 6 month frequency $ 525.00

PRELIMINARY INTRODUCTORY VISIT $ 25.00
      (TIME ELEMENT: One to Three Hours)
As a courtesy to anyone seeking more
information about programming procedures
as they might relate to their particular
circumstances. This $25.00 charge is non-
refundable but is deducted from the Initial
fee.

TRANSFER FAMILIES - Initial Charge $ 425.00
      (TIME ELEMENT: One very lengthy day and
a portion of the night; or portions of
two days)

Patterning fee schedule 1982.

Crawl attempts on inclined plane patterning exercise.

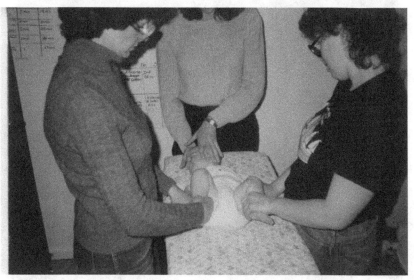

Homologous seesaw patterning exercise.

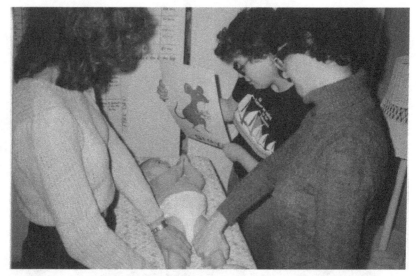

Horizontal Leg Unlocking patterning
exercise—Late Grandma Rita in purple.

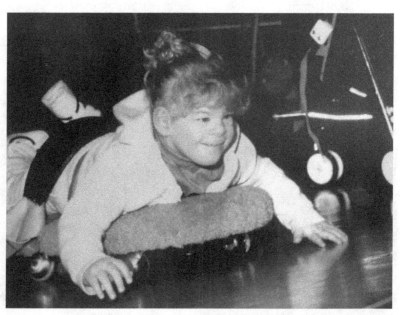

Physical therapy exercise at United Cerebral
Palsy Association, 1984 (currently Aspire
of WNY) Specialized School.

INITIAL FUNCTIONAL NEUROLOGICAL SENSORIMOTOR DEVELOPMENTAL EVALUATION AND
INSTRUCTION IN SUGGESTED TECHNIQUE TREATMENT PROCEDURES FOR JESSICA LAYNE
RUBIN - THURSDAY & FRIDAY - DECEMBER 9TH & 10TH, 1982 - IN THE RUBIN HOME
IN TONOWANDA, NEW YORK BY GENE LEWIS-ATLANTA, GEORGIA ....

SESSION "A" - Patterning Segment - Requires 4 persons preferably

1.   6 MIN - VESTIBULAR STIMULUS - Swing in Sheet or Blanket
        1.   1 MIN - Swing side to side movement - 30 round trips
        2.   ½ MIN - Place on floor - flashcard exposure; geometric
                     patterns, simple pictures, math dot cards, and
                     later words, etc.
                     Begin with minimum exposures 6 seconds X 5 cards
                     Later increase to 3 seconds X 10 cards
        3.   1 MIN - Swing head to toe movement - 30 round trips
        4.   ½ MIN - Place on floor - repeat flashcard exposure as in
                     Item #2 (preferably using the same cards as above
                     during this segment)
        5.   1 MIN - Bounce - 40 and up to 75 times
        6.   ½ MIN - Place on floor - repeat flashcard exposure as in
                     Items #2, #4.
        7.   1 MIN - Swing side to side movement- 30 round trips (repeat
                     of Item #1).

2.   5 MIN - HOMOLOGOUS (all 4 limbs move simultaneously) SEE SAW - TOGETHER
        AND APART WITH HEAD MOVING CENTER, SIDE, CENTER, OPPOSITE SIDE.
        Starting Position: (also Apart Position): Head is flat and
        centered; both arms extend back and over head, palms of hands
        face the ceiling, patterner's finger inpalm in Jessica's hand;
        both legs extend down and arein alignment with hips.
        Together Position: Head alternately rotated toone side; arms go
        downward to sides and legs flexed upward still maintaining
        alignment with hips.

        (do not confuse with homolateral patterning on back where legs
        move out at right angles and arms at right angles instead of
        up and down movement)

     1 MIN - BRUSH HANDS AND FEET - 20 Times - Brush 2,3 - IT IS IMPORTANT
        THAT EVERY ONE BRUSH THEIR LIMB WITH EVERY ONE ELSE FOR THE IM-
        PACT OF THE STIMULUS TO BE REGISTERED. TRY NOT TO GET OUT OF
        SEQUENCE, IF YOU DO, STOP AND START OVER. The 2,3 allows time
        for the stimulus to travel and be received and processed by the
        brain centers
        BRUSH, 2,3, BRUSH 2,3, 3,2,3, 4,2,3, 5,2,3, etc.

     1 MIN - PUSH - PULL - TWIST - TWIST - & JOINT VIBRATIONS
        Wrists & ankles - 5 X 5 sets
        (if things are going smoothly, it would be good to extend this
        to 2 MIN or 5 X 6 Sets).

     5 MIN - HOMOLATERAL - (Same side matches, i.e. one arm and one leg on
        one side if flexed at right angle while opposite side is straight.
        SEE-SAW - TOGETHER & APART
        1.   Boths arms up; both legs down; head centered
        2.   Rt arm down rt leg up, head rotates to rt.
        3.   Rt arm up rt leg down, head rotates tocenter
        4.   Lt arm down lt leg up, head rotates tolt.
        5.   Lt arm up, lt leg down, head rotatesto center.

Patterning, page 1.

PAGE -2- RE: JESSICA LAYNE RUBIN - INITIAL EVALUATION - 9TH & 10TH DEC. 82

6.　2 MIN - HORIZONTAL LEG UNLOCKING WHILE LYING ON BACK & HEAD PERSON EX-POSES JESSICA TO FLASHCARDS WHILE PERSONS ON SIDES FLEX HER LEGS. One leg is straight and relaxed while opposite leg is flexed out, then up, and at this point push down slightly just above the flexed knww and push up slightly on the ball of the foot to stretch the heel cord areaand move downward to the straight and relaxed or extended leg position.

7.　5 MIN - HOMOLATERAL (same side matches) PATTERNING ON BACK - Limbs are different from Together & apart in that the flexed arm and leg on one side are at right angles. (This is different from Items #2, #5)(You also alternate smoothly from side to side and do not return to Midline as in #2, & #5)

8.　1 MIN - BRUSH HANDS & FEET - 20 Times, Brush, 2,3, etc. (Repeat of Item #3).

9.　1 MIN - PUSH - PULL - TWIST - TWIST & JOINT VIBRATIONS elbows & knees - 5 X 3 sets (if things are going smoothly, it would be good to extend this to 2 MIN or 5 X 6 sets).

TURN OVER ON STOMACH ON TOP OF PATTERNING TABLE

10.　5 MIN - HOMOLATERAL PATTERNING ON STOMACH - (Same as Item #7, except on stomach in lieu of being on back).

11.　3 MIN - (OR LONGER) CRAWL ATTEMPTS - with reflex stimulus up under seat while on floor on mat or preferably on satin piece of materal stretched over the carpet. (GOOD IDEA TO HOOK SATIN MATERIAL ENDS FROM BASEBOARD TO BASEBOARD ACROSS THE ROOM) for a mobility runner. In this way you will be able to keep up with the number of feet Jessica movesor covers per day. (IT IS IMPORTANT TO KEEP UP WITH THE FOOTAGE OF MOVEMENT SHE MAKES).

12.　3 MIN - (OR LONGER) CRAWL ATTEMPTS - ON THE SLIDE OR INCLINED PLANE - Begin with heighth of 36 inches - place Jessica at the top of the slide - any movement she makes will facilitate forward mobility downhill - do not assist if she is engaged in movement but assists if she stops movement for over 15 seconds. AS JESSICA MOVES MORE RAPIDLY THEN SLOWLY LOWER THE SLIDE INCH BY INCH SO SHE WILL NOT BE DISCOURAGED AND HAVE TO WORK TOO HARD TO MOVE, BUT DON'T LET IT BECOME TO THE POINT BY WHICH WHEN YOU PLACE HER ON THE SLIDE SHE JUST SLIDES DOWNHILL. (with no effort)

13.　10 MIN - BREAK -- if/as necessary - also change diapers, etc.

TIME ELEMENT: 38 MINUTES OF ACTIVITY PLUS 10 MINUTE BREAK - 48 MIN TOTAL TOTAL OF 50 MIN IF YOU INCREASE THE PUSH - PULL - TWIST - TWIST AND JOINT VIBRATIONS AS MENTIONED IN ITEMS 4 & 9 from 1 to 2 MIN

Patterning, page 2.

December 17, 1982

Dear Friends:

The members of Temple Sinai have been presented with the opportunity to perform a true and beautiful Mitzvah!

A member of our congregation needs the assistance of some of our other members not financially, but physically and morally.

One of our younger family members has an eight-month old child who is developmentally delayed. The mother and father of the child desperately need volunteers to help their infant improve, through the Doman-Delacato program of "patterning". Each volunteer is needed for 2½ hours each week to help the infant move her arms and legs, or to show flash cards to the infant.

No experience in such work is necessary, as the parents are trained and prepared to teach volunteers how to assist.

Your response may open the door to a full and natural life for another human being. Help a child! Help this child now!

If you are interested in helping this family, please call them during the day at 835-1216. You will enrich their lives and also your own.

Sincerely,

Betty Goodman, President

Joseph D. Herzog, Rabbi

Letter from Rabbi asking for
patterning volunteers 1982.

CHAPTER 4

Reality Sets In

Our world wasn't always blissful in the Rubin household, and although our love and devotion to Jessica was unfaltering, sadness and despair often tapped on our shoulders. We really didn't know what the hell we were doing, and the stress of multitudes of unknowns weighed heavily on our hearts and marriage.

This can be seen in a journal entry from December 14, 1982. (The language was politically correct at that time, and since it's a personal note, I did not change it.)

I think that Jessie's handicap is sinking in. The road ahead is very blurred because:

1. Jessie is so young; we don't know the extent.

2. There are so many things to do I don't know which to do first or if what I do is the right choice.

> I must stop worrying about imaginary problems and focus on the real issues. Everybody tells me how strong I am; sometimes I feel that maybe I am the weakest. I think about many unimportant things instead of focusing on the real problems. I am getting a lot done and I'm realistic about what is going on but in private time, I think of unimportant things. Anyway, I spoke to Dr. C. and he believes patterning won't hurt Jessie. He doesn't agree with it in theory. I am going to call this week and start Monday! A NEW DIRECTION.[2]

It's thirty-seven years later, and I don't recall the sadness and uncertainty that I was experiencing; my recollections are more positive. It's humbling to find that letter, and my young self probably had the wisdom to keep those thoughts hidden in a drawer so that I would find it sometime in the future.

I do recollect my hypochondria as mentioned in the previous chapters, and I strongly believe that was my coping mechanism. If I worried about moles, lumps, bumps, colds, and possible pneumonia, then I didn't have to focus on what the future held with Jessica. It was a simple strategy

---

[2] This entry was written prior to starting patterning.

that got me through in the absence of professional counseling—something, in hindsight, I should have pursued.

Our marriage suffered during this time. Not only were we struggling with Jess, but in 1982, we also had financial struggles and a (perceived) lack of support. Although Mitch's Grandma Rose helped me with countless hours of loving assistance, at times I felt sorry for myself.

Grandma Rose, as everyone referred to her, was a brilliant, strong, resourceful woman. I met Grandma the first week Mitch and I were dating. We were at the University of Miami, and his grandparents wintered in the South Beach area before it was art deco and cool; it was 1976. I barely knew Mitch, and he was already bringing me to meet the matriarch of the family, which sent waves of anxiety through my body. We drove in Mitch's car, which had no air conditioning, and we were in Florida. I recall shoving my arms out the window because I didn't want to have pit stains under my arms. When we arrived, Grandma Rose and Grandpa Morris received me with open arms. I think they loved me at first because Mitch was bringing home a Jewish girl, but eventually I became loved as a family member for other reasons.

Rose Iskowitz was born at the turn of the twentieth century when few career and educational options were available to women. She came from a remote town in Hungary and immigrated with her family to New York City. Grandma Rose was about five feet four, had curly blonde hair, a prominent nose, and a beautiful smile. She always stood tall and was a presence if not in stature, then in personality and intellect. She was a devoted CNN follower and strikingly advocated for legalization of marijuana; she thought using pot should not be a criminal offense.

Grandma was a forward thinker and way ahead of her time. Perhaps if Grandma were born today, she would be the first female president. Politics aside, her true claims to fame were her potato latkes (crispy potato pancakes) and kindlach. Kindlach is a Hungarian pastry filled with walnuts and cinnamon, rolled in the shape of a long tube, and cut into slices after baking. (I researched this term, and the closest I got was Hungarian nut rolls or beigli.) I wish I had the time and patience to learn how to make these delicacies as she did, but I was too immersed with Jess to think of cooking.

In the 1980s and early 1990s, Grandma Rose was extremely helpful with Jessica until Jess grew too heavy for her to lift. She was always a set of helping hands. I knew at the time if I was ever lucky enough to have grandchildren, I would model my actions based on Grandma Rose. Mitch and I would always be thankful for the kindness and nonjudgmental, pure love that Grandma shared with our children and family.

I also had a lot of emotional and physical support from my beloved friend, Barbara. I met Barbara in an unlikely setting as she rarely went to the "fancy" store where we had our first encounter. I was shopping with my mother-in-law, Rita. (Rita loved to spoil me with shopping, and I was a willing and eager participant.) One day, I met a woman with an infant snuggled on her chest (I think we called the contraption a Snugli at the time), and we started chatting. We spoke quite a while before I bid her *adieu* and went to find Rita. As soon as I reached Rita, she asked if I got the woman's number. I was somewhat horrified. "How can I get her number? Is this a bar? Am I picking up random shoppers?" Rita, who never insisted I do anything, was adamant that I go back and get this woman's number. So I followed instructions and asked Barb for her number. Barb and I met almost every day after that first meeting, and I always felt that the universe was looking out for me because Jess was diagnosed a month after I met Barbara. She supported me then and to this day.

Mitch and I are not what you'd call two peas in a pod; we are the people that the old TV show "Green Acres" was written about. He is outdoors, and I am city. Or at least that's how we started out, although over the years we have morphed into appreciating city and hinterlands. (Correction: *I* have morphed into appreciating hinterlands; Mitch will visit a city and enjoy the visit, but we own a home in a rural community.) Mitch's mom always told me that he was never a baby, and he marched to his own drum— her words and my agreement—and willfully did his own thing. To this day, Mitch looks at requests or questions as if you are telling him what to do, so as a savvy experienced doctor of "Mitchology," I have learned to make sure that he thinks that he came up with the idea. And sometimes it even works.

There are a few key philosophies that Mitch and I have in common. Our first and foremost is love and devotion to our family. They come first. The second, or perhaps part of our first commonality, is our united commitment to Jess. We didn't argue about her care, our willingness to bring Jess everywhere, our pride in Jess, and our protectiveness. We are on the same page, and that has sustained my love for Mitch throughout the years. We are in agreement with respect to the importance of all family, giving to others (sometimes he's a bit more giving than me), doing the right thing, cherishing friendships, and appreciating what we have. I believe Mitch and Jess taught me to be a better person, and for that I am grateful.

As beautiful as the previously mentioned may sound, we certainly struggled as is depicted in another yellowed but saved journal entry from 1983 as follows (with my current commentary in brackets):

> Mitch and I do not get along at all. We are on two different wavelengths. With all I'm doing with the baby (i.e., hospital appointments, infant stimulation [this was before federal law for Early Intervention], patterning, and maintaining forty volunteers, he still complained his shirts weren't ironed [this makes my current self laugh—ironing shirts, really?] and the house is a mess (it isn't mainly because I have to keep it clean for the volunteers?). He also says I pay too much attention to Jessie and not enough to him [he was probably right]. He's such a child. He doesn't play enough with Jess at all unless I force it. Then he watches TV with her in his arms. He gave her a bath

today for the first time in nine months! And of course, he had the biggest fight with me before he did it. He takes off work but has never patterned, he doesn't even ask how it went. He never compliments me. He is more concerned with sports and himself than me or Jess. He doesn't realize the mental and physical strain this is. His answer is, "You want to go to work for me?" He thinks this is MY job alone and I get no support from him. It's hard enough getting everything organized with Jess, but having a shitty, horrible marriage makes it 1,000,000 times worse!

Life was often difficult for us. We were young when we had Jess, and although that was beneficial in terms of our energy level, we also were immature. Imagine yourself at the age of twenty-four raising a child with severe disabilities and complex medical issues; it was overwhelming to us and our marriage. I repeatedly wanted more help from Mitch, and the more that I asked—Mitch would say nagged—the more he retreated.

Mitch likes to be in charge, and so do I. When we attended meetings about Jessica, I preferred to lead the discussions; after all, in my never humble opinion, I spent more time caring for Jess and communicating with teachers, therapists, and physicians. Mitch's opinion was that I didn't let him talk, and so he stopped attending most appointments and conferences. He is right; I did take control, and at the time, I thought it was my call to be in charge. I was wrong, and did Mitch a huge disservice by not playing as a team.

Before you start looking for the divorce chapter in this memoir, another spoiler alert: we are still married. As I write this, Mitch and I have been married forty years; we have made it work and, after all these years, love each other and the life we created. Marriage, as most of life, has its ups and downs, ebbs and flows. A person can feel as down as I did in the paragraph above, yet remain committed to the marriage. Marriage and love are only perfect in movies on the Hallmark channel and romance novels. The rest of us go from loveliness to ugliness—sometimes in the same day. I encourage you not to give up; if there are still moments of joy and love, continue to persevere, and it will pay off in the end.

Grandma Rose, 1983.

Barb and Jess, 1990.

Jess and Barb, 2016.

CHAPTER 5

We Did Everything— it Just Took Longer

W e eventually got quite savvy at taking care of Jess and started talking about increasing our family. There was always the looming question, What if this happens again? I subscribed to the scholarly philosophy of "Have faith, knock on wood, and hopefully it will all work out." Mitch and I don't always agree on the topic of having faith; however, we both do knock on wood. Knocking on wood is a custom that supposedly staves off bad luck. People usually knock on wood after they have good fortune and want it to continue. Our intellect tells us this is ridiculous, yet we just can't stop ourselves from continuing the tradition. We are proactive rather than passive when it comes to making things happen, but I sometimes hope that a higher being is also in our corner.

Many couples, if their marriage survives having a child with a significant disability, choose not to have other children. It's understandable when you have already experienced more hardship than expected. Concerns range from the aforementioned, Will this happen again? to, How will I give my first child the intense care they need with another baby in the family? Families worry about giving their second child the care they need when they already have their hands full. Increased financial pressure adds tension to an already fatigued marriage. Most young families worry about money whether or not they have a child with disabilities. I often comment that if we had waited until we could afford kids, we would be having them when we were in our fifties.

For some unexplained reason, Mitch and I were not fearful of having a second child and embraced the idea of a growing family. This makes no sense knowing my personality, which ruminates on all that can and presumably will go wrong, even with the wood knocking.

I quickly became pregnant with Baby 2. It was December 1983, and my due date was August 1984. We chose to have an amniocentesis to determine the genetic makeup of the fetus. The lab was specifically looking at the fifth chromosome because we were still under the mistaken impression that was the location of Jessica's deletion. The amniocentesis was terrifying because there was an increased risk of miscarriage, plus I was already feeling

Baby 2 kick. I told Mitch that, regardless of the outcome, I was not going to end this pregnancy. Convincing myself that the test was only to prepare us for whatever the outcome was going to be, I agreed to the procedure.

My greatest concern following the amniocentesis was miscarriage, but after we felt confident that I had no ill effects from the testing, we started thinking about what the potential answers could mean to our family. Each day centered around the question, What will we do if Baby 2 has the same deletion?

While I was pregnant with Baby 2, both my grandparents passed away within two weeks of each other. They were married more than sixty years. My grandfather's funeral, in Long Island, happened to be the same day I was getting the results of the amniocentesis. Mitch was on his annual fishing trip and unable to return in time, so I flew to New York alone, disheartened that I would be getting the news without him by my side.

After the funeral, I went to my cousin Andrea's house and called the doctor. Lifting the wall phone in the kitchen, I hesitantly dialed the office, knowing that after waiting numerous weeks for the results, this was the moment that would give us information that would shape the rest of our lives.

The last few moments of anticipation were painful. My grandfather's funeral was emotionally draining, and I wasn't sure I could handle more bad news. The receptionist answered and put me on hold for what felt like a lifetime. The nurse came back on the phone and revealed that the results of the amniocentesis were normal. It was great news!

I think we were somewhat convinced it wouldn't happen again, but you never truly know.

Thirty-six years later I was speaking to my cousin Andrea, and she commented, "I'll always remember you making that call." Mitch was not with me for that call, but I recently realized that I was not alone, as my cousin retains vivid memories of the day and the emotion.

July, a month before my due date, was the beginning of Jessica's summer school program where she was transitioning into a new special education preschool. The program was twenty minutes from our home, and I drove Jess back and forth every day. I carried her on my nine-month pregnant belly as we trudged into the classroom for the daily 2.5-hour sessions. I didn't realize that parental attendance was not required in preschool and often wondered why the other parents weren't hanging around with me as in previous programs.

Jessica's teacher, Nan, was too kind to kick me out. The great benefit of so much quality time together was our blossoming friendship—the kind of friends who become family. We became such good friends that many years later, Mitch walked Nan down the aisle when she married her husband, John. Nan became a key person in our lives, who helped us when nobody else was able to be there. There have been a few people who stand out in our life, and Nan is one of our heroes because she came to our rescue after Baby 2 was born.

I would love to say that Baby 2's delivery was smooth, but that wasn't the case. The umbilical cord was wrapped around his neck, and the doctor needed to remove the baby as fast as possible to prevent harm. The delivery was successful, but in the process, I was cut so deeply from the episiotomy that the doctor wanted to put me under general anesthesia to stitch me back together. I refused and told him that if I could have a baby without drugs, I was certainly not going to be put under for the repair. The bottom line was that our beautiful baby boy with the biggest eyes and longest lashes in the land was delivered safely; we named him Alexander Leo.

A few days after delivery I started to hemorrhage, and my mother-in-law rushed me to the hospital. It turns out there was still placenta in my womb, and I needed bed rest for several days. Bed rest—were they kidding? At the same time, Mitch hurt his leg (sports-related injury) and was using crutches, so essentially, he was useless for baby care. My parents were in Florida, and my in-laws were not available; we were stranded. Until I remembered Nan. One quick call was all it took for Nan to come to our rescue. She expertly took care of both kids, slept over, cooked for us, and even baked cookies. She made the difference between complete meltdown and survival, and we will forever be grateful.

What was it like having a typical child after Jessica? For one thing, it was astounding. Every gurgle or movement Alex made was astonishing to us. My friend once commented that Alex was going to think he was the king because we were so awed at every milestone; he was our personal miracle. On the flip side, I couldn't relax and was constantly inspecting Alex for delays, disability, disease, and disaster. Fortunately, he remembers none of this.

Meanwhile, my school driving with Jessica ended, and she had to take a bus to preschool. Envision putting a two-year-old on a bus every day. We had to have faith that the people who were caring for our daughter were making good decisions and doing the right thing. We had one frightening bus incident. Jessica's transport was somewhat consistent with her scheduled drop-off; however, one day she was extremely late. The thought of not knowing the whereabouts of our defenseless, nonverbal (a condition of most two-year-olds), and vulnerable toddler threw me into a frenzy. I called the bus company and school who said they would find her location. I don't recall how long we waited for Jess to arrive home, but in mommy time it was way too long. I am embarrassed to say that when she arrived home, I quickly opened her diaper to check her private parts to see if anything looked different. Even in the 1980s, my first thought went down that treacherous path. Fortunately, Jess was fine. The new driver said he was lost and apologized for the delay. And we had to have trust to put her back on the bus the next day.

We survived having Baby 2, and things were going relatively smoothly. So we thought, "Let's make it a trifecta." Mitch and I often spoke about the possibility of a third child. We dreamed of having three children and a dog. But now a third child took on a greater significance because we didn't want Alex to feel solely responsible for Jessica's well-being once Mitch and I were no longer on the planet. Baby 3 was planned for our future, but we were still struggling with Jess and Alex and thought we should wait longer for our third.

Mitch reminded me of Baby 3's conception (youngest child—you may want to skip to the next chapter). I have no memory of the beginning, but Mitch's memories are quite clear. Of course, it was sports related as so many of his stories are. He started by telling me it was the day he quit golf. Mitch recalls a lot of drinking after his "last" day of golf and getting a ride home to share his joy with me. That is how Baby 3 was conceived, and oddly, the one who was not drunk has no recollection of the event.

The next part of our story is still vivid to me. I received the news that I was pregnant again and raced to where Mitch was working. I had the kids in the car, so he came outside to see why I was visiting. I didn't have a great reveal or cute way of telling him the news. I blurted out, "I'm pregnant!"

Mitch's reaction was not one of joy. He did not go in for the big hug and twirl me around as in the movies. Instead, he looked at me like a deer in the headlights and turned back and walked into the store. He was in shock; I am not sure why. Didn't he recall his postgolf adventure? There I stood, devastated about his reaction. Of course, he later came around and apologized for his reaction.

Carly Sara was born April 23, 1987, and from the moment she came into the world, she was in charge. Whereas Alex excelled in language at a young age, Carly excelled at walking and movement.

Three kids in five years; three kids in diapers—one child who couldn't walk, one who refused to walk, and one who wanted to walk everywhere. We were constantly stopped and asked if we had triplets; they did not look alike, but they appeared to be close in age. I think we were an interesting group that confounded those around us.

How did we get around? As I mentioned, Alex did not like to walk, and before Carly could walk, I used a double-length stroller (no side-by-side in those days). Our stroller was a heavy, long piece of equipment that was difficult to assemble, steer, and maneuver. Jess and Alex rode in the stroller, and Carly was placed in a knapsack on my back and off we would go.

Time passed, and Carly became somewhat mobile. I recall taking Alex to nursery school with Jess still in a stroller. Alex was forced to walk holding my hand as Carly followed in a baby walker behind us. We were a sight. Those baby walkers are no longer made because kids were injured, but I am thankful that in the late 1980s we were oblivious to all the potential hazards.

It is almost thirty-one years later as I write this chapter and reminisce about those days. Carly and Alex are both married and have blessed us with grandchildren. Not too long ago, I asked them what it was like growing up with Jess and if they felt as if their childhood was impaired in any way. Independent of each other, both Alex and Carly had the same impression of their childhood. Both siblings insisted that they did not miss out on any activities, saying, "We did everything—it just took longer."

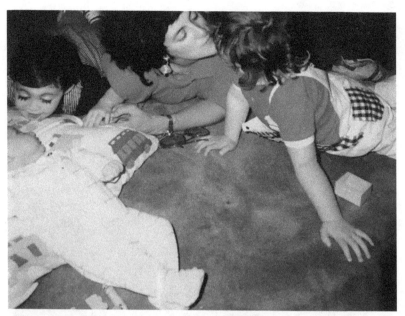

Vickie Jessica Alex Carly, 1987.

Grandma Rita, Great-grandma
Rose, Alex, and Jess, 1985.

Great-grandma Rose, Alex, Carly, and Jess, 1990.

Mitch with Jess and Alex in double stroller, 1984.

Vickie with Jess and Alex in double stroller, 1984.

Jess and Alex, 1985.

Mitch walking Nan down the aisle, 1987.

Nan, John, Vickie, Mitch, and Jess—Jess was
the flower girl at Nan and John's wedding.

Vickie, Mitch, Jess, and Alex, August 1984.

CHAPTER 6

Panic and Milestones and Tears—Oh My!

I was always baffled about my reaction to having Jess. As I mentioned in chapter 2, I yearned to release my pain with tears, but none came. I never completely understood why I didn't cry. I think about this personal quirkiness often because I find it hard to cry about a lot of things that most people easily succumb to, yet I can tear up instantly at a sad commercial or when I feel wronged by somebody. It's not that I don't feel like crying or don't feel the same intensity of sadness. I just can't cry when it's—for lack of a better word—expected.

When Jess received her diagnosis, I didn't weep, sob, or wail; instead, I got busy. I was completely immersed in figuring out how to fix Jess, planning each day around all the therapies and supports she required. Did I think I was going to repair all her disabilities? The extensive amount of therapy and strategies would suggest that was the goal. All I know is that I wanted to be on track to achieve milestones quickly.

I think my expression of grief came out in the form of panic attacks. This led to an unwelcome cycle of hyperventilation, dizziness, and more hyperventilation. These episodes occurred at random times. Waiting in line at the supermarket was a popular spot for my panic to erupt. Along with panic, I experienced an increase of hypochondria. Unquestionably, I was a bit over the top, and I still insist it would have been easier to cry.

I was so afraid of something happening to me because who else would take care of Jess and later Alex and Carly? Maybe if I could have cried more, I would have gone to the doctor less. It's hard to know.

The daily "what if" thoughts were a recurring struggle. I eventually went to a counselor and was able to get on track. I still have a lot of the same fears and trepidation, but it's a reasonable amount, at least in my opinion. I suspect there are those who know me well who would beg to differ.

Having spoken to other families and having read posts, articles, and books, I know that it is hard not to compare your child with developmental disabilities to their typical developing peers. For example, when your friend's children start kindergarten, have their first crush, get their first job, get married, and eventually have their own children, it's difficult not to compare. The everyday ability of speaking, walking, sitting, feeding oneself, and using the bathroom independently are evidence for comparison when you have young children. It's normal to long for your children to experience the same milestones as their peers.

If we had felt jealousy toward our friend's children's typical development, we would not have had any friends. I have seen the result of comparisons. Some people who are unable to get pregnant slowly lose their friends with children because of the constant reminder of their loss. Families of children with disabilities may start to shun friends with kids the same age. It can feel like a constant reminder.

We often attribute not feeling the milestone misery described above to our joy of having more children. Alex and Carly gave us those experiences and left us in awe of everyday normal occurrences and development.

Mitch and I always looked at Jess as unique. She was following her own path, and we couldn't compare her to others. Jess was so far delayed that there was no point in looking at what others her age were achieving. I sometimes think that if Jess were less impeded, we may have had more angst about what she should be doing. But as in the TV show "Survivor", we basically voted ourselves off the island and started our own island with unique rules, expectations, and milestones.

Mitch and I had a couple of milestones to conquer, and one of them was Jessica's first wheelchair. What did it feel like to decide to get a wheelchair for our five-year-old daughter?

Getting a wheelchair is a big step. Ordering a wheelchair, in our minds, meant crossing the line from, "Maybe one day Jess will walk" to "We are giving up." Jess was small, and we were able to use a kid's stroller for a longer time than it recommends on the stroller directions. Who reads that stuff anyway?

Meanwhile, the physical therapists were gently encouraging us to explore the chair. "It comes in really cute colors," was a frequent sales pitch. I am not sure if something specific eventually turned the tide or if it was the growing necessity and reality, but we finally agreed to order the chair.

The chair arrived on a warm spring day while we were playing outside. Jessica's new chair was bright red and truly adorable, if one can describe a wheelchair as cute and adorable. We placed Jess in her glossy new chariot and realized at once that this was the right decision. She was comfortable and sitting tall and proud.

Jess was over five years old when she received her first chair, which shows that as much as we thought we accepted the diagnosis and all that accompanied it, there was still some hope for a miracle. The chair, at the time, somewhat squashed that dream.

In hindsight, getting a wheelchair does not mean that a person will *never* walk. It means that they will be more comfortable and their body will be supported appropriately while still working on other skills. We just didn't know that yet.

Over the years, Jess had many cool and colorful wheelchairs; we still order bright colors to match her bright smile. She has sported a purple chair, metallic blue with shimmer, and of course, several red ones. Jess can maneuver her wheelchair, but only when she wants to. In fact, I have seen her navigate a three-point turn to get to the table for dessert. Jess, like her mother, loves chocolate! Conversely, at other moments, she has stared at me as if to say, "You expect me to move this chair by myself?"

Did Jess ever learn to walk? That depends on one's definition of walking. Eventually, Jess was able to use a walker to stand and take several steps, and she is able to walk if we hold both her hands, stand behind her, bent over into a ninety-degree angle, straining our backs as we carry a lot of her weight. As Jess gained weight and our backs aged, we did not cover a lot of territory.

Our next milestone to overcome in the world of denial was the matching wheelchair van. When I was in college, my parents gave me a Datsun 280Z sports car. I kept the car until we had Alex and needed a back seat. Prior to that, Jess and I tooled around town in my hot rod. One thing I made clear to Mitch before we had kids was that I never wanted to drive a station wagon or similar suburban vehicle, which would have included minivans, but they weren't invented yet. Obviously, my priorities still needed some tweaking. I guess karma's a bitch because not only did but we also end up with a few minivans, we eventually ended up with a wheelchair minivan. This demonstrates how life and family changes your priorities because I was thrilled and grateful that we were able to purchase this vehicle. Arrogantly planning that I would only have a cool car reminds me of the old Yiddish adage, *"Mann tracht, un gott lacht"*—*"Man plans and God laughs."*

Our initial wheelchair van was a beige Plymouth Voyager. It was sent to a specialist to "Pimp my Ride" (for those who remember the MTV show). The company removed the middle row of seats and added supports, harnesses, side-door wheelchair ramp, and other adaptations that are beyond my scope of automobile expertise.

We were truly excited to get our new ride. Ah—the ease of getting Jess around town, the fun it would be to quickly arrive, and perhaps not be late for everything.

One story that highlights our transportation learning curve was an outing with our friend, Sheryl. Let me preface this story with a statement that our family loves ice cream. Many of our celebrations and everyday routines include ice cream.

The day we received the van, Carly, Jess, and I invited our friend Sheryl to the local ice cream stand in our new modified van. Sheryl got in the front seat as I started to attach Jess to all the harnesses and clamps and hooks. Time was ticking, and I was sweating profusely, trying to secure Jess to the van. Sheryl, meanwhile, was joking that if she knew it was going to take so long, she would have brought an overnight bag. She continued, "Perhaps I should call my boss to tell her I will be late for work tomorrow morning." Sheryl's monologue only made it worse because I was laughing so hard, I couldn't do anything. Thirty minutes passed before Jessica's wheelchair was secured to the van. We finally got ice cream, and it got easier. Most of the experiences that start out as insurmountable eventually became doable; unfortunately, that is often another lesson learned in hindsight.

Over the years, the van became a lifesaver and helped protect our backs and ease travel. And I did cry the first day we received the van, but not tears of sorrow. It was tears of laughter because of Sheryl's relentless banter while I was struggling to attach Jess. We still laugh about this—the best medicine for overcoming adversity.

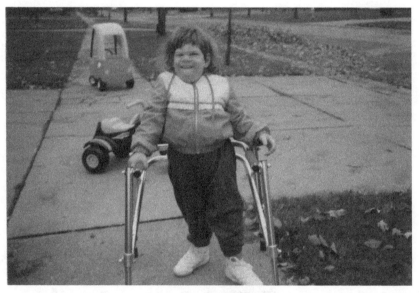

Jess using her rollator.

CHAPTER 7

Breaking the Code

Jessica, at age twelve, always appeared alert and aware of her surroundings, yet there was no back-and-forth verbal communication. I couldn't ask Jess to make a choice. Things we take for granted such as saying "yes" or "no," "I'm happy," "I'm hurt," "I'm hungry," or "I'm sad" were trapped inside of Jess. We were desperate to find a way to release her thoughts.

Jess worked on sign language at school, and we tried picture boards plus other alternative communication strategies that were not successful. The doctors reminded us that Jessica's IQ was so low that she was not motivated to communicate. They insisted that she didn't understand the relationship of communicative cause and effect, meaning a request provides a response that fulfills a need. We didn't agree because when we looked in Jessica's eyes, a light shined, and we needed to know how to retrieve what was in her mind. How could we break her code?

One afternoon my neighbor, Bea, told me of an eighteen-year-old boy who was using a new form of communication called facilitated communication (FC). This method was helping individuals with autism who were nonverbal to interact with meaningful conversation. She encouraged me to call and get more information. I still had patterning in my memory and was hesitant to start another experimental treatment. It took me two months to initiate a call to get more information about FC. Would this be yet another experiment that didn't work? Was it fair to raise our hopes only to be disappointed? Finally, we decided to call because if there was a possibility of giving Jess the ability to make a choice, we had to at least give it a chance.

I contacted the mother of the eighteen-year-old boy, and she told me all about facilitated communication.[3] She explained its simplicity whereby the facilitator physically supports another person and helps that individual point to pictures or words. I started helping Jess by isolating her index finger, which she still does independently to this day. Next, I supported her forearm, and when I felt Jessica's hand move toward a letter, I offered slight resistance. The resistance helped to stabilize Jessica's hand so that she was

---

[3] Facilitated communication was developed in Australia by Rosemary Crossley and brought to the United State by Douglas Biklen. For more information, see https://link.springer.com/referencework entry/10.1007%2F978-1-4419-1698-3_773.

able to accurately select a letter. It felt a bit like an old-school Ouija board. An important note is that the facilitator does not assist in selecting the letters, he or she only provides gentle support so the individual can freely choose the letters or word.

I was fortunate that a two-day seminar in FC was offered the following week at the University at Buffalo, and there was room for me to attend. The session was filled with teachers; I was the only parent. The mother I had spoken to was one of the presenters, and her son was willing to let everyone facilitate with him. He wanted us to feel the power of facilitated communication so that we would be able to open the communication doors for others. Once you tried it, it was hard not to believe that this was an authentic strategy.

When Jess came home from school that afternoon, I was ready and waiting with two index cards. "Yes" was written on one card, and "No" on the other. I isolated Jessica's index finger and slightly restrained her hand, as I was taught, and asked Jess if she wanted chocolate milk (her favorite). She pushed my hand toward the Yes card. I then asked Jess if she wanted water (least favorite), and Jess indicated No. I felt elation, disbelief, belief, skepticism—could this be a miracle? Did Jess know how to read but had no way of showing us prior to FC? The idea was far-fetched, but was it also possible? My mind was a whirl of questions. Did I want this so much that I was unintentionally guiding her hand toward what I thought to be Jessica's answer? Facilitator guidance, deliberate or not, was a persistent criticism of FC and one that plagued me and other family members.

We worked on FC for more than a year. Jess started spelling family members' names; she knew the date and was able to identify numbers. At one point during an evaluation, she moved her fingers toward the word "hi." Imagine after twelve years, a simple greeting, a life changed forever. From this point on, we included Jessica in fifth-grade math and discovered that she could multiply, add, and subtract. Jess was also able to identify money, and she began to learn more about the world around her. We were amazed at all the information Jessica had absorbed incidentally, without direct instruction, and we realized that Jessica's possibilities were limitless.

Mitch and I never imagined that Jess had this level of cognition. One day I sat down with Jess and asked if there was anything she wanted to tell me, "I love you, Mom" was her message. I had been waiting twelve years to hear that.

So as Paul Harvey (a beloved radio personality from the 1970s to 2009) would say, "And now the rest of the story." My parents were visiting one weekend and my dad and I decided to test FC. I guess I still had a bit of skepticism. We played the FC game of telephone where my father whispered something into Jessica's ear, and I asked her to facilitate the message to me. It never worked, although we tried a lot. I came up with excuses that maybe Jessica didn't get the game or maybe she didn't want to play or maybe she was pulling one over on us. Alas, this became the beginning of the end for FC for us as other incongruities started to show up. I requested that the school ask Jessica what she did over the weekend without them having prior knowledge, and the answer was rarely correct. Some of her clinicians still believed that FC was a viable tool for Jess, and I believe that for some folks it truly works, but we ultimately stopped using this method as her only mode of communication.

Facilitated communication helped Jess learn to isolate her index finger independently, which led to another mode of communication. This was the early 1990s, and we didn't have iPhones or tablets with apps. The DynaVox[4] was the newest voice output device used for talking. The DynaVox resembled a touch screen tablet, but it was much larger and heavier. It had tiered pages that contained different vocabulary for numerous situations such as food, recreation, social situations, and other life experiences.

Our school district purchased this extremely costly device for Jessica, and we worked on conversing through technology. Jess was very interested in her DynaVox, but not for communication. One of the icons on her board was for the song, "Blue Hawaii," sung in a dreadful digital rendition. My family still groans at the mention of this song. Jess became obsessed with the tune; she refused to click on "Yes" and "No" icons because she only wanted to tap on "Blue Hawaii." Jess was so adept at the DynaVox that when her clinicians moved the "Blue Hawaii" icon to a different page, Jess was able to click through the other pages and files on her board until she successfully found her beloved melody. Again, Jess didn't consistently communicate her wants and needs for everyday requests, but she did show us how much she could do with proper motivation. We were

---

[4] See the description of DynaVox at https://en.wikipedia.org/wiki/DynaVox.

disappointed about the failure of facilitated communication, but still amazed at her point-and-search skills.

I learned several things during this process. Jess communicates, but not with words. She lets me know that chocolate milk is her favorite with beautiful smiles and voracious drinking. She lets us know when she is happy— we just look at her face. She also lets us know when she is pissed off. Most important, she always lets us know how much she loves us with her hugs, glee when we walk into the room, kisses, screeches, and facial expressions. Jessica has her own language, and if you take the time, you can break the code.

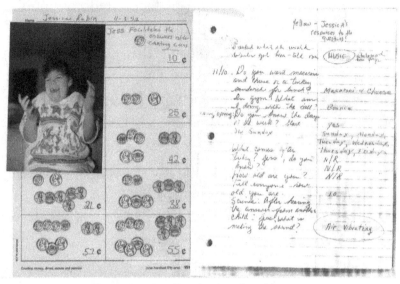

Jessica's schoolwork completed using
facilitated communication, 1992.

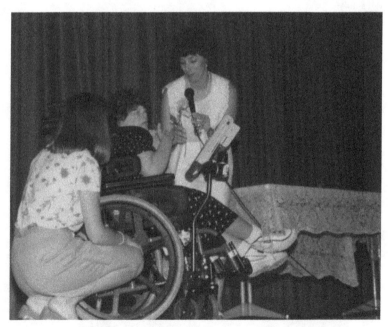

Jess using her DynaVox while she receives 8th grade
communication award for her effort, 1993.

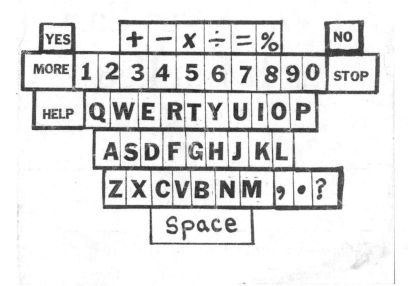

Simple facilitated communication spelling board.

CHAPTER 8

It Wasn't as Easy as It Looked

This book is entitled *Raising Jess: A Story of Hope*, but that doesn't mean everything was easy or that we were smiling and joyful all the time. There were—and still are—a lot of trying times.

Sometimes I think we made it look too easy. We may have given the illusion of having it all together, but it was a hot mess trying to do anything. Our motto (mentioned in a previous chapter) was, "We will do everything—it will just take longer." We tried to live by those words.

One story highlights some of the challenges we faced. Throughout my childhood, Christmas was the best day of the year. We celebrated *Christmukah* (our Hanukah celebration on Christmas Day) by meeting with family, eating copious amounts of food, and of course, the presents! I don't know if my childhood brain is lying to my adult brain, but the memory includes mountains of gifts. This tradition started with my mother's family and continued until my Aunt Claire passed away in 2010. I always knew my Aunt Claire and Uncle Shelly were the heart and soul of the party, and when they were no longer around, us "kids" would not be able to continue the tradition.

Spending Christmas in Long Island was nonnegotiable for me, but we had three young children, including one in a wheelchair, who needed assistance with everything. To complicate matters, in the 1980s and '90s, Mitch co-owned a retail store, and everyone knows that retail and Christmas are like bread and butter; in fact, it was our bread and butter for the entire year. Each Christmas Eve, Mitch closed the store at 4:00 p.m., and the family piled into the van and drove more than seven hours to Long Island with our specialized equipment, gifts, food, clothing, and diapers. The following day, we celebrated with extended family and then packed up the car and drove home. Retail requires you to be open the day after Christmas for all the returns. We did this for many, many years. Occasionally, we would say to the downstate family, "How about Christmas in Buffalo this year?" The response was typically how hard it would be for them, how long the drive was, where would they sleep, and other similar excuses. We tried to host it in Buffalo one time, and the only folks who showed up were my parents, my brother Keith, and his family. Did the extended family realize how much effort it took us to get there and take care of Jess? Maybe not. Perhaps we didn't complain enough or made it look too easy. Or perhaps it's true about New Yorkers, which I still consider myself to be, that the city is the center of the universe and all those other places—such as Buffalo—are the Wild West that one only reads about.

Another example was our constant tardiness. One of the requirements of going out at night with friends was to be on time. I am sad to say that we never mastered this concept. Mitch and I could be dressed and ready to go when we would realize that Jess needed changing or some other assistance. This happened often, and so another twenty minutes was added to our departure and we showed up late. We used Jess as our excuse, but I think because we often made it look as if we were so together, our friends never truly believed our outlandish claims.

My third example is a well-meaning invitation. I was alone with Jess and had just finished bathing her, giving her medicine, and finally putting her to bed for the night. As I walked out of her room, my phone rang and a friend called to say, "Hey, let's go for ice cream." As you already know, I rarely turn down ice cream, but had to decline because as I told my very smart "PhD" friend, I had just put Jess to bed. Her reply was, "Just get her out of bed and meet at the ice cream shop." This was a close friend who knew Jess well, yet she had no concept of the amount of work it would take to "just get Jess out of bed and meet for ice cream." Dressing Jessica, getting the wheelchair and wheelchair van going, putting on new diapers, heavy lifting, and more would have taken so much time and energy. I declined, but I have thought about this conversation often and wondered if we made it look too easy.

Toilet training didn't only last several months as with most toddlers; it was ongoing and only moderately successful. We often brought a child's potty with us and would stop every hour, no matter what we were doing, and place the toilet in the van for Jess. There was a point when we were brave enough to try underwear rather than diapers, but we were never fully successful. The process was extremely time-consuming, annoying to our other kids, and sometimes made it a lot easier to stay home than to venture out. Eventually, we had to choose quality of life for the family rather than toilet training out of the home. Jess, as an adult, still wears briefs but appears to understand the concept of using the toilet and is often successful.

Going out for family adventures or errands was like packing for an overnight stay. It was equivalent to what new parents bring when they take their infants out in the community, except this didn't end at two or three years of age. Our bag included bibs, multiple changes of clothes, briefs, wipes, pureed food, juice boxes, plastic bags, a wheelchair, and our strong arms and backs for lifting. When Carly and Alex were babies, it doubled and tripled the amount of supplies. At one point, we had three kids in diapers.

Another constant fear was the risk of choking. This is still a significant concern today because Jessica has a very high pallet and very poor chewing skills. She had a fluoroscopy (an X-ray that shows the route her food passes from lips to esophagus) to determine that she chews a bit but not enough for foods that have a chewy or hard consistency. Our dinner table often was disrupted by loud coughing, choking sounds, and Jess turning red. I am still not used to this. I have a rule in our house, "No choking allowed," but Jess, like her dad, is not a rule follower. You may be wondering why we feed Jess food that will induce choking. On the contrary, her food is soft and of a consistency that matches her skill; however, this does not guarantee that Jess will not make choking sounds.

Family vacations were another hurdle for our family. Mitch and I recently realized that we never developed the habit of traveling with other families, as our friends did; it was too difficult for us. Instead, Mitch and I took separate vacations with Alex or Carly. There is an advantage to this Plan B as Carly and I developed an annual ski trip. We have traveled to western as well as eastern ski resorts. We rarely see other mother-daughter duos on our ski trips, and it makes us feel like we are cool (or maybe it just makes *me* feel cool). Alex and I share a love of Broadway, and he and I traveled to New York City to see shows. We still relish this love of theater today. Mitch took the kids on separate outings, usually a sporting theme such as canoe trips or baseball games. We made it work.

Overnight respite services funded by New York State changed our lives. Respite provides parents with short-term care services for their child. In New York State, especially in the 1990s and early 2000s, we had the opportunity of using a lot of overnight services. The amount of respite that we enjoyed is no longer available because of funding. When Jess became older, she spent one or two weekends each month at a respite center. It was not easy to trust that other caregivers were going to be able to identify seizures, feed Jessica the right food consistency, know when she was sick, and make sure that she was not sitting in a corner doing nothing. We eventually began to have confidence with the centers that we frequented, first by starting with very short visits and slowly increasing the time. Respite changed our lives, and we believe it was the reason we were able to care for Jess in our home for so long.

Jess also had two surgeries that were not typical for most children. The first was to correct a dislocated hip. We struggled with the decision to repair her hip, but after weighing the risks versus benefits, we decided to have the surgery that took place in 1990 when she had just turned eight years old. This was a few years after the discovery of HIV/AIDS, and I was very concerned about blood transfusions for Jessica. Transfusions were common with hip surgeries, and we couldn't be 100 percent sure that the blood wasn't tainted. Parents were not allowed to donate blood because there was a rare chance of rejection. I decided to get directed donors, people we chose to have blood waiting for Jess if she would need a transfusion. I asked people whom I knew well and found three willing volunteers from our temple.

May 1, 1990 was a date I will always remember. Jessica's surgery initially appeared to go well. When we were finally allowed to visit Jess in recovery, I instantly noticed how pale she looked. Her lips were the color of her ashen skin. I asked the nurse to check her vitals. She tried to get her blood pressure with one machine and determined that since it had no reading, the machine was broken. She went to get a second machine, which also didn't seem to work. It never occurred to her that the blood pressure machines were working and that Jess was crashing. Through some higher intervention, her doctor happened to come into the room to check on Jess. He took one look at her and called a code. She was losing too much blood. I did not handle this well and ran into the hall screaming. A few minutes later a priest came to find me, and I thought, *This is it—he is here to give me the bad news*. I was somewhat relieved when he said, "I just want to say a prayer for your daughter." All prayers, all denominations were welcome. Jess was saved; the blood that was generously donated was used, and her hip was successfully repaired. Many months later at a follow-up visit we decided, along with the doctor, that we would not risk this surgery again.

Jess's second major surgery, when she was almost twenty-one years old, started out quite differently. She had been experiencing intense itching for which we could not figure out the source. The doctors thought it was behavior. (When you have a child with a disability, so many symptoms are attributed to behavior.) Next, her doctor thought perhaps Jess had scabies and we had to treat her with a toxic solvent and hold her hands for close to twenty-four hours so that she wouldn't put them in her mouth. When she continued to scratch, they suggested it was a possible reaction to her seizure medications. Meanwhile, a friend told me a story about her cousin who had intense itching which turned out to be caused by her gallbladder. We called Jessica's pediatrician and spoke to a new young doctor who had recently joined the practice. He refused to agree to a sonogram of Jessica's gallbladder, stating that she had no symptoms that would suggest a gallbladder problem. This dilemma called for a voice more persuasive than mine, so I got Mitch to call back. The doctor finally agreed to the ultrasound. Mitch has a tone that is more "convincing" than mine.

The ultrasound revealed numerous large gallstones, and we were told to go immediately to the hospital for surgery. It was March 2007, seventeen years after her last surgery, but not enough time had passed for us to willingly put Jess through this again. We had no choice. My greatest recollection of this day was when the surgeon came out after hours of surgery and asked us to join him in the small conversation room. I hope you don't know the room I am talking about because this is not a room where you receive good news. The doctor explained that Jessica's gallbladder was attached solidly to her liver, he described it like cement, and that her body structure was atypical. The head surgeon said they had called another surgical expert from Roswell Cancer Institute (again they came to the rescue) to assist with the surgery. My next thought after wondering whether Jessica was going to survive this was wondering if she had cancer.

The surgeon assured us that she did not have cancer and that she was going to be fine. We had to believe this, but it was not an easy task. I went into Jessica's hospital room and lay in the fetal position for what felt like hours. Mitch waited in the waiting room for word. Finally, Jessica came out of surgery, and it was successful. Her post-op recovery was far easier than with the hip and she eventually went home to recuperate.

I received a phone call from the young pediatrician the day after Jessica's surgery. He apologized for not acknowledging our concerns and listening to us. He told me that he learned a valuable lesson and that he would not dismiss families concerns and suggestions in the future. I know this must have been a hard call from the pediatrician, and we have always appreciated his gesture. We remained with the practice, and this doctor became a beloved medical provider in our community.

The moral of our story is that we were able to laugh at some of it—some of it may have been inappropriate laughter, but it worked better than self-pity. We overcame a lot, endured much, dreaded some, but survived it all.

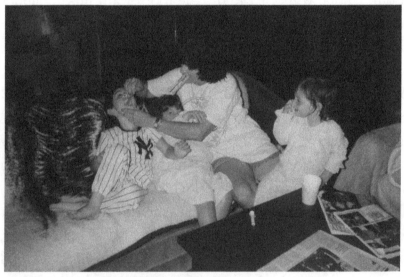

Brushing all three kids' teeth at the same time.
Carly's toothbrush was in my mouth, she was
waiting her turn. It was like having triplets.

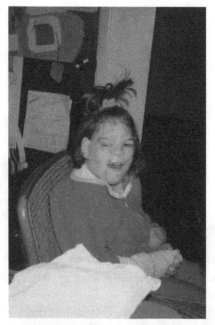

Jess finally got chickenpox, mid-1990s.

Jessica postoperative from hip surgery, 1990.

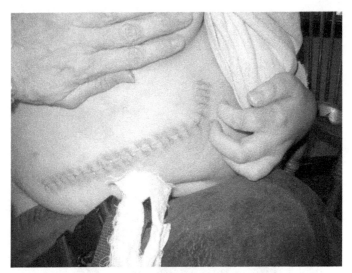

Staples after gallbladder surgery, March 2003.

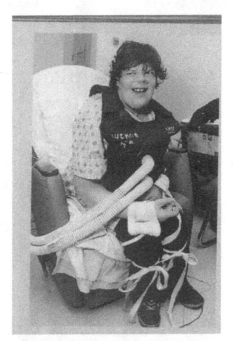

Postoperative respiratory assistance device
used to support lung health. Jess suffered a
collapsed lung one day after surgery.

CHAPTER 9

Seizures Suck!

Jessica's first seizure struck in 1982 and will always be memorable, not only because of the seizure, but also because of the circumstances.

Did you ever have a moment when you knew someone or something intervened?

I always suspected that Jess was having some type of seizure. Perhaps it was mother's intuition or just common sense, but when I saw Jess "startle" for no apparent reason, it concerned me. I recall a visit to her doctor who tried to convince me that Jess was not having a seizure. He went on to suggest that she was hearing (and startling to) sounds that I didn't hear. I thought, *Huh? You mean like a dog?* I walked out of the office with that explanation.

Several months later, Jess developed an upper respiratory infection and was given penicillin for her symptoms. This was back in the days when antibiotics were the first choice rather than today's last resort. In 1982 it was not common knowledge that antibiotic resistant organisms would one day render many treatments ineffective. Doctors blissfully gave antibiotics for everything—and they worked.

The first day Jess had penicillin, she was under one year of age. Jess and I were outside in front of our house when a car stopped on our driveway. I initially didn't know who it was, but in those days, you walked over to the car rather than second-guessing with suspicion. Our unexpected visitor, whom I will refer to as John, a work acquaintance from my husband's store, happened to be driving down the street and saw me standing by our house. We chatted a moment outside. I eventually invited him inside while thinking to myself that this was odd; he had never been to our house, and I don't recall ever talking with him outside of our work environment.

I placed Jess in the front hall, still in her 1980s car seat (which would probably get us arrested by today's safety standards) as John and I walked through the house. It was a small house; we were gone less than two minutes. Upon returning to the front hall, I was shocked to find Jess with her eyes bulging, thick drool coming from her mouth, and a blue discoloration on her upper lip. She was unresponsive. Immediately I panicked.

Here is where the moment of intervention enters. It turns out that John, a Vietnam War veteran, had experience with medical emergencies. He sprang into action by calling 911, keeping me calm, and waiting with me for the ambulance. I believe that John's timely visit may not have been a coincidence. His assistance made the difference between total chaos and prompt emergency care.

Jess and I raced to the hospital by ambulance, and I regret to say that the remainder of this story is a blur. I think that happens a lot with parents; perhaps it's nature's way of making sure that the population continues. If you ask a mom for the horrific details of her birthing experience, you may get a tidbit of information here and there, but the true intensity of it is mostly gone in that fuzzy section of the brain. I recall my daughter Carly saying to me that she barely has memories of the first six months of our grandson's childhood; it all begins when he started sleeping through the night. I believe Mother Nature wants us to keep procreating, which would not happen so frequently if our memories were crystal clear.

Back to the hospital. Unfortunately, this was the first of many emergency room visits because of seizures. It never got easier; I always panicked. Thankfully, Mitch maintains a cool head and was an amazing dad and husband during these trying moments. Mitch sprang into action, often giving me tasks while waiting for an ambulance so that I was busy getting ready rather than falling to pieces.

The term for Jessica's first seizure was febrile, which is a fancy word for fever. The not-so-technical definition is a convulsion in a child caused by a sudden increase in body temperature, often preceded by an infection. Febrile seizures can happen in children who do not have a seizure condition as well. The seizure usually doesn't last very long, but in momma minutes, it's an eternity.

I never allowed Jess to have penicillin again. Is she allergic? Probably not, but the seizure happened within moments of her first dosage, and it terrified me to risk repeating this event.

Jess developed a seizure condition, and she has numerous types of seizures[5] (myoclonic, petit mall, tonic-clonic) that are mostly controlled with medication. When Jess was younger, I added pharmacist to my credentials in the broadest sense of the term. I determined that when Jess had numerous seizures, I called the neurologist, and he suggested that we increase her medicine a bit here and there. After many years of tweaking her dosage, I started to do it myself, with the doctor's approval. In my nonmedical opinion, the prescription and dosage of seizure medication sometimes felt like a crap shoot—let's try this or maybe that, or how about this plus that? This is not a criticism of the medical field, but an observation of how much we still don't know. And please do not try this at home!

I'm not overly religious and don't subscribe to the philosophy that a higher being chose us to be Jessica's parents, but I sometimes question if there is a master coordinator somewhere who puts people in the right place at the right time. The seizure incident is not the only time this has happened to us. In a previous chapter, I mentioned the chance meeting with my lifelong friend, Barbara.

---

[5] For more information on seizures, see https://www.epilepsy.com/learn/types-seizures.

When Jess was first diagnosed, somebody gave me the book, *When Bad Things Happen to Good People* by Harold S. Kushner.[6] Rabbi Kushner's young son was diagnosed with a degenerative disease, which led him to question and doubt a higher being. My interpretation of his message was that God does not orchestrate tragedies, heartache, or disaster, but he does surround you with people who help you navigate the circumstances. Humans have responsibility to maintain this earth, but perhaps the higher being assists with giving the capacity of selflessness and compassion so that we are there for our friends, family, and sometimes even strangers. This is a personalized and simplified version. If you want the true wisdom, please refer to the book as noted below.

I am not a rabbi, and I never went to religious school; however, I do have faith. I believe there is something beyond our existence here on earth. Whatever the source of compassionate friends and family, strangers, or acquaintances who are in the right place at the right time, it is not as important as the fact that there are people who care so much that they go the extra mile for our family. That is one of many beautiful silver linings of our journey.

---

[6] Harold S. Kushner, *When Bad Things Happen to Good People* (Random House Inc., 1981).

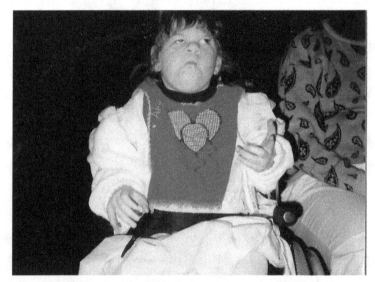

Photo captured of Jess having a myoclonic seizure.

CHAPTER 10

A New Direction

I am going to step back from the kids to my college days, also known as the disco era of the late '70s. It was 1975, and I was a freshman at the University of Miami in Florida. My only goals were to attend college, find a husband, and get married. Living in New York City was also in my postgraduation plan; however, I had no career strategy to sustain my fantasy city lifestyle.

I met my future roommate, Tami, during our first semester. She was an education major and forty-three years later is still a cherished friend. We were roommates from the second semester of our freshman year until graduation.

Tami and I met Mitch on the first day of our second semester; it was 1976. We had moved into a new dorm, and as we entered the lobby, I ran into a friend from Long Island named Jay, who happened to be standing with a skinny, long-haired dude who he introduced as Mitch from Buffalo. Tami and I said a quick hi and fled to the elevator.

The next day, a few friends and I were invited to a party off campus, but we didn't have a car. It was 1976, and we didn't have cell phones, Ubers, or Lyft; the only way to travel was to hitch, at least in our minds. We arrived safely at the party and stayed for several hours. It was close to midnight when I stepped out to the patio and saw Mitch, who I knew had a car, and asked him to tell me the time. (Mitch later opened a watch store called Watch World[7] in 1980 and always loved that one of my first lines to him was, "What time is it?") We started dating immediately after this second-chance meeting.

I needed to declare a major during my second semester, and neither hitching, drinking, disco dancing, or moving to New York City was in the university's catalog. Mitch encouraged me to go into elementary education like his mom, Rita. This career path made perfect sense to *him*, and I figured, "Why not?" Eventually I developed an interest in the field and earned a 4.0 in every class from second semester up to graduation. I recalled the time one professor asked me if I was interested in pursuing special education, and my reply was, "Oh no, I have no patience for that!" Interesting how life works.

Mitch graduated in December 1978, five months before my planned graduation in May. He returned to Buffalo to

---

[7] http://www.watchworldbuffalo.com/

start working with his father, so we wrote letters and talked on the phone every day. In February he flew back to Miami, and we went out to dinner. He was so awkward during the evening that I was wondering if our relationship had changed now that we were apart. On the contrary, and unbeknownst to me, Mitch was trying to gather the courage to pop the question.

Mitch had flown to New York prior to his flight to Miami to ask my dad for my hand in marriage. My dad's reply was something to the effect that, "As long as you can keep her in the style that she is accustomed." That should have been enough to send Mitch running for the hills. To his credit, he continued to Miami with the ring and two celebratory newspapers he'd had printed in New York.

We sat at the restaurant in awkward silence until Mitch hesitantly asked, "Will you marry me?" He also gave me a couple of caveats, one being if I didn't say yes, that I should drive him back to the airport immediately. The second caveat (which I have no memory of, but Mitch is very clear) had to do with him going on annual fishing trips. After our negotiations were completed, I agreed. Mitch reached down to his briefcase that he had brought into the restaurant and pulled out two faux *New York Times* newspapers. The headlines read, "Vickie and Mitch Engaged!" I guess Mitch really did know I would say yes. We were married seven months after graduation.

I recently visited Tami and told her about this book. Throughout undergraduate school, Tami always teased me about my copious writing and note taking. She didn't take notes and always excelled in school. I had to write everything down, almost word for word. Tami admitted to me on our recent visit that maybe all that writing was a good thing because it led to this book. Validation after forty-three years!

Travel forward with me to 1991. We had three children, and I felt a need to learn all I could about providing Jessica with the best education. I felt I would be more equipped to advocate for Jess with a master's degree in special education with a specialty in severe and profound intellectual disability (in those days the course catalog still used the term *retardation*).

I was accepted to Buffalo State College Graduate program in 1991. I was unable to commit to more than a single class a semester because we had only one reliable aide for Jess one afternoon per week. It took a decade to receive my master's in exceptional education while caring for three children.

I was very disciplined, or maybe it's the OCD thing again, and was keen on completing schoolwork every morning after the kids went to school. I am still very productive in the morning, which is the reason that this book can be written. I am at my creative and clever peak around 6:00 a.m., and it all goes downhill from there.

I loved exceptional education and was completely immersed in the course work. It seemed that every class related to Jessica, and I was eating up the information.

All the early morning work paid off as my school career ended on a high note. While writing this chapter, I found my name on the President's Award page at Buffalo State

College from 2001. Below is a portion of the announcement from the website:

> Vickie L. Rubin will receive the President's Medal for Outstanding Graduate... Rubin graduates with a Master of Science in Exceptional Education and is the recipient of this year's Bernard Yormak Award for Outstanding Graduate Student in the Exceptional Education Department.[8]

When I started my master's in 1991, I still had no career direction but knew one day I would find a job, at a maximum, to help support our family and at a minimum to justify my parent's investment of too much money at University of Miami and Buffalo State College. They kept their promise to pay for my schooling no matter how old I was when attending. I am extremely appreciative of their support.

My career path in Buffalo was not linear, and from 1979 to 1998, I went from one position to another. Most paid jobs were part-time, and none were truly satisfying. My focus was on raising the three children while they were young.

In 1998, the kids were more settled, and I had reliable personal care aides for Jess. It was time to look for a paying job.

I rifled through the classified ads of our local newspaper and came across a posting from a famous chocolate company that was looking for a local representative. I like

---

[8] http://bscintra.buffalostate.edu/bulletin/archives/00_01/april26_01.html

chocolate; in fact, I love chocolate, and I knew this could be my career. The job included benefits and flexible hours, which was a must considering Jessica's needs and the fact that aides often did not show up on time or at all. I went for my first interview.

On February 22, 1998, as I was waiting to hear if I was going to be the next female Willy Wonka, I continued to search the newspaper ads and came across a small posting from Buffalo Children's Hospital. The posting was from the Early Childhood Direction Center (ECDC) and described an opening for a teacher. It was a temporary flexible position, and the candidate had to have a preschool special education background. I was still in graduate school, but my undergraduate degree included a minor in early childhood.

I decided to call the director of ECDC for an interview. The new grant-funded position was titled Parent Educator, and my role would be to assist families to understand the preschool special education system in our six-county region. Astonishingly, I was hired on the spot. I was a bit stunned and replied that I needed to go home and think it over.

Later that day, I described the position to Mitch, who said that this job was made for me. It was the perfect match, and I had to take it. It was my calling! I felt inadequate, and although I had so much experience with Jessica, I wasn't sure I knew enough to get paid to help others navigate the special education system, but I took the job and left my dreams of chocolate behind.

This job led me down a new career path that I never could have predicted; it was light years away from my vision in 1979. In 2001, I became the director of the Early Childhood Direction Center[9] and managed our New York State grant-funded department at Buffalo Children's Hospital. This opportunity provided me with the knowledge and experience to advocate for children and teach parents and professionals in our region and state. I retired in 2017 after eighteen years. Unfortunately, the ECDC lost its funding on June 30, 2019, forty years after NYS initiated the grant.

The ability to make a difference in the lives of others, and to get paid, was a dream come true—if I could have dreamed that far. I attribute taking this path to Mitch, who has always been my cheerleader and has encouraged me to stretch more than I think I am able. Jessica inspired me to help others in similar situations, to try to give other families hope that they, too, would survive and thrive, and to understand that we do not have control of what happens to us or our family, but we do have control of how we respond.

---

[9] For more information about Early Childhood Direction Centers, go to the following sites:
https://www.health.ny.gov/community/infants_children/early_intervention/transition/appendix_b.htm
https://www.kaleidahealth.org/Childrens/pdf/WCHOB-563-ECDCbrochure.pdf

Vickie and Mitch engaged, 1979.

Mitch and Vickie—University of Miami
(Florida) Graduation Day, 1979.

Original job posting for Parent Educator at
the Early Childhood Direction Center, 1998.

The Western Region is fortunate to have an Early Childhood Direction Center that provides stellar leadership and assists others in networking on behalf of providing quality special education programming.

Photo of Jessica and Vickie in Children's Hospital of Buffalo Annual Report.

CHAPTER 11

Inclusion

Jessica's public education encompassed numerous schools and classrooms. She started in the infant program at Robert Warner Rehabilitation Center (Children's Hospital of Buffalo), moved to a special education classroom in a center for children with special needs, and at age five, went to a school district Boards of Cooperative Education Services (BOCES) program. The program was more than a thirty-minute drive from our home. Jess remained in that program, which moved from district to district, until she was twelve.

Meanwhile, I was working with our district to include Jessica in our neighborhood's middle school. Like the line from the old TV show "Cheers," we wanted everyone to know her name. Jess lived in our town, yet the teens her age only saw her as the girl in a wheelchair who made a lot of noise. Nobody knew who she was. This was going to change.

I became very involved with the school district and volunteered to sit on their Committee on Special Education (CSE) comprised of a group of individuals who made decisions about the services that children within our district with special needs would receive. I was one of several parent representatives that helped families understand the special education process. The volunteer position provided me with an opportunity to help others, and I learned firsthand about the creative services available in our district.

At Jessica's CSE meetings, we planned for her entry into the neighborhood middle school. There was a lot of groundwork involved because Jess was the first student in the school who used a wheelchair. The amount of support that she needed in a typical classroom was extraordinary. Yet the district and teachers were up to the task, as were we. Was Jessica ready for the change?

I went into the school prior to Jessica's first day and presented a disability awareness program to the other students in the classroom. I explained her differences, but more importantly, I told them how Jessica was like them. "She also loves chocolate, music, and movies. Jessica has siblings and dogs, and she lives in the neighborhood." I then answered questions from the students as honestly as possible.

One of the first times I knew inclusion was a success was when I took Jessica to our local grocery store. Some of her school peers were in the store, and instead of getting the who-is-that-in-the-wheelchair glare, we received a welcome. The kids came up to Jess, greeted her by name, and said, "She goes to my school." This gesture brought tears to my eyes.

Receiving services in a middle school classroom meant that we had to make some trades. Whereas Jessica was receiving training on socialization and other vital skills in typical classrooms, her toileting and other skills of daily living were put on the back burner. It was not easy to work on feeding and toileting in an inclusive setting. We knew this going in, and we were willing to take the risk. And we had Mary Ellen, who was Jessica's assistant and treasured friend on our side. Mary Ellen made sure that Jess was getting all she could from her middle school experience.

Jessica was embraced by the students, so much so that she was invited to a schoolmate's Bar Mitzvah. I was invited too, but only to assist Jess; she was truly the invitee, and it warmed our hearts that Jess was accepted.

Jess remained in middle school for four years, but as the years passed, we saw the writing on the wall. High school was going to be too hard for full inclusion. There was not the same amount of flexibility in the classrooms, and we believed that Jess could not get the same benefits of camaraderie and socialization in a high school math or science classroom.

Once again, we went back to the district CSE and determined that Jessica could benefit from a special education BOCES class, but this time, the classroom was in our neighborhood district. Her teacher, Les Currier, set up a program that we called reverse inclusion whereby the high school students who were interested went into Jessica's classroom and assisted. Les created a club called the Pride Club (which had a different connotation in the 1990s than it does now), and many students joined and participated. Most importantly, they wanted to be involved.

During high school, Jess joined chorus and participated in other typical high school activities. She thrived in the classes with the help of her teacher, Les, and her one-to-one aide, Val. While Les was the leader, Val was the day-to-day support that made this a successful setting. Val not only provided all personal care, but she also worked on academics, socialization skills, and participated in after-school activities. Val was pivotal in the success of the program.

Jessica attended every dance sponsored by her high school. She experienced field trips and school functions. Jess arrived at school each day with her lunch, notebook, and a smile. She remained in Les's class until she turned twenty-one.

Prior to the end of Jessica's senior year, Mitch and I received a note from the principal that Jessica was to receive an award. The evening was held in June, and we attended along with our friend Ellen and the family. The award ceremony was very long, and it was hot. Hours passed, and Jessica's name was not called. We started to question if there was an error and began to feel uncomfortable because we had invited everyone to attend.

Finally, the principal stood up to deliver the last award of the evening. It was the Principal's Award. He started by saying, "This student overcomes hardships every day of her life." He spoke of the student's courage and enthusiasm for school. He went on to say that although this student had many challenges every single day, she still came to school with joy and a smile and brought that joy to all those around her. "This award goes to Jessica Rubin!"

Thunderous applause filled the room as we rolled up to the stage to receive Jessica's award. Yes, it was worth the wait; yes, Jess earned that award; and yes, her district saw beyond the wheelchair and the disabilities to the young woman who brought joy to those around her.

One month later, Jessica participated in high school graduation. She used her walker to ambulate across the stage, and I walked by her side. That's where I have always been and always plan to be as we continue our path. We did not feel sadness or sorrow for Jess and all the things she missed out on in high school. Jess earned her place among the graduating class of Williamsville East High School, and our family celebrated Jessica's graduation with pride and joy.

Jess and Josh.

Jess and Val.

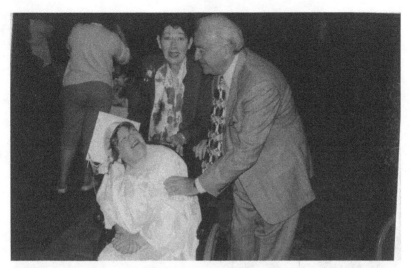

Grandpa Marty and Grandma
Norma at Jessica's graduation.

Graduation from Williamsville East High School,
2003.
Family and friends attended.

Vickie with Jessica graduating from Board of
Cooperative Education Services (BOCES), 2003

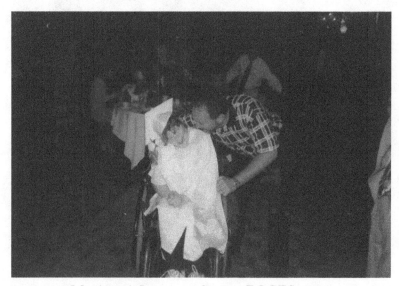

Mitch with Jessica graduating BOCES, 2003

Jess walked the stage for her graduation
with assist from Vickie, 2002.

Jessica formal graduation photo.

CHAPTER 12

Jessica's Bat Mitzvah

When Jess was an infant and we discovered that she had multiple disabilities, our plans for her future were altered. One milestone we never thought would occur was the celebration of Jessica's Bat Mitzvah, a traditional Jewish passage to adulthood for thirteen-year-old boys and girls. (*Bar* refers to coming of age for Jewish boys, and *Bat* is used for coming of age for Jewish girls.) How does a child who doesn't speak, cannot read, and doesn't understand Hebrew have the potential to become a Bat Mitzvah girl?

A sermon our rabbi delivered at temple during Rosh Hashanah[10] opened the door of possibility for Jessica to celebrate her Bat Mitzvah.

Rabbi Barry Schwartz's sermon described a thirteen-year-old boy with severe disabilities who celebrated his Bar Mitzvah. Although this young man could not speak or read, he was able to show his spiritualism through music. This struck a chord (pun intended) with Mitch and me.

Rabbi Schwartz had previously informed us privately about the young man and suggested that we consider a similar celebration for Jessica. We put the thought in the back of our minds, but never seriously considered it until hearing the sermon and the inspiring story again. We decided to meet with Rabbi Schwartz to discuss the possibilities of a Bat Mitzvah for Jessica.

The first thing we wanted to understand was the different ways one could become a Bat Mitzvah girl. Did we want this so much for our child that we were creating a watered-down version of the real thing—in other words, faking it? Rabbi Schwartz quickly alleviated that doubt when he explained that all Jewish people become a Bar or Bat Mitzvah boy or girl regardless of their Jewish education. It simply means that you are old enough to take on the responsibility to learn and practice your religion *to the best of your ability*. This milestone occurs when you reach the age of thirteen.

Once we realized that learning Hebrew and reading from the Torah (sacred religious scrolls) were not absolute

---

[10] Rosh Hashana is the Jewish New Year and the beginning of the ten-day holiest period of the Jewish year.

prerequisites for becoming a Bat Mitzvah girl, we became intrigued with the prospect of Jessica, and us, experiencing this wonderful opportunity.

To prepare for this day, Jessica started to attend Junior Congregation at Temple Sinai[11] on Sundays. She became familiar with the rituals of the service, the familiar tunes of prayer, and the other children in our congregation. We considered this a part of Jessica's education. Had we realized that Jewish study could have been possible for Jess, we could have included her in Hebrew School at a younger age. Since we only had one year to prepare, we believed Junior Congregation was the best place to start.

We brainstormed with our rabbi to find a match between Jessica's strengths and a meaningful service. Music immediately came to mind. When Jessica attended Friday night services, she clapped and beamed whenever the rabbi or cantorial soloist, the late Susan Wehle,[12] sang a song or prayer. Anyone who watched Jessica during these times could attest that she felt the spirit of religion through music. We decided to incorporate as much music as possible into Jessica's service.

---

[11] Temple Sinai in Amherst, New York, merged with Temple Beth Am in Williamsville, New York, on July 1, 2012. The temple is now called Congregation Shir Shalom.

[12] The late Susan Wehle added spirit and beauty to the service. Tragically in 2009, Susan passed away with forty-nine other souls on continental flight 3407. (See the article https://www.jweekly.com/2009/02/20/plane-crash-near-buffalo-takes-life-of-beloved-cantor/.) Susan was loved by everyone she encountered. She was a person who gave so much of herself and expected nothing in return.

Mitch and I immediately thought of our friend Glenn Colton, a well-known local musician. One website describes Glenn as "a blend of '70s AM Gold, a little Jimmy Buffett, with just a dash of Mr. Rogers thrown in for good measure."[13] Although Glenn is not Jewish, we knew he was perfect for the ceremony. We asked him to sing individually and along with our clergy. The song themes had to do with friendship, acceptance, peace, and love.

Our son Alex, who was twelve at the time, wrote and performed a song that spoke of his pride and excitement as Jess celebrated her Bat Mitzvah. There was not a dry eye in the house after he sang. Jessica beamed with pride and joy throughout the entire service.

The ceremony was held on a Friday night rather than the traditional Saturday morning Bat Mitzvah service. Rabbi Schwartz felt this was an appropriate time since Jessica was not reading from the Torah and we could be more flexible on a Friday with the service.

Did Jessica know what was going on? You'd better believe she did! The expression on her face, the maturity she showed that evening, and the way she grabbed Rabbi Schwartz's hand as he blessed her revealed to the whole congregation the extent of Jessica's joy during her ceremony.

Another testament to the scope of Jessica's understanding of the service was a small detail about her head covering (*yarmulke*). Typically, the Bat Mitzvah celebrant wears a yarmulke. Jessica does not like to wear hats. To this day, she reaches up and throws her hat to the ground. We

---

[13] For more information on Glenn Colton, see https://store.cdbaby.com/artist/GlennColton.

were a bit apprehensive about Jessica keeping the yarmulke on her head.

Meanwhile, our friend Ellen Palmer and her family had a different opinion and set upon a mission to buy a beautiful yarmulke and *tallit* (prayer shawl) for Jessica. They drove to a neighboring city and found a magnificent set made from a cream-colored fabric with pink and silver threading. Jess did not attempt to remove her yarmulke or tallit the entire service—a small detail that most of the congregation wouldn't have noticed, but our immediate family knew this was significant.

Jessica used her DynaVox to recite the Shema, one of the holiest prayers. I wonder how many DynaVoxes were programmed to participate in a Bat Mitzvah? I entered the English transliteration of the sacred Hebrew prayer into Jessica's device and used a picture of the Torah as the icon. The plan was for Jessica to independently touch the icon (in front of more than two hundred people), resulting in the computer reciting the sacred prayer. Our younger daughter Carly, assisted by chanting the prayer after Jessica finished her portion.

Jessica had practiced this at school and home, but we were not sure she could do this in front of a crowd. We rolled her wheelchair to the front of the congregation and hoped for the best. Jessica immediately pushed the correct icon and was so excited that she did it again and again.

Our whole family was involved in the Bat Mitzvah. Alex and Carly recited prayers in Hebrew. Grandparents helped as well as friends; it was truly a group effort. The communal participation and love in the room was palpable. One eighty-nine-year-old gentleman who attended the ceremony told us that in all his years he had never been to a more meaningful and beautiful ceremony.

Mitch and I each gave a speech about the meaning of this day and the pride we felt for Jessica. Mitch's poignant words told the story of the journey to this moment:

> This is a truly special evening for all of us. People are here to honor Jess, Vickie, myself, and our family. I would like to acknowledge the true appreciation we have to those of you who have made even the smallest difference in Jessica's life. To those of you who come here to honor Jess, who know her smile and warmth, hugs, and laughs—a special thank-you. This day is so meaningful to our family, an evening where Jessica is celebrated and honored for being a Bat Mitzvah as any other Jewish girl of thirteen. We have come a long way as a family and a community to have total acceptance. It's not easy; it is many times a great effort, but the outcome of inclusion, acceptance, honor, and love is worth the effort... My late mother would have been in her glory tonight. She, more than anyone I know, could appreciate everything leading up to tonight.

My speech spoke of the coincidence of the portion of the Torah and Jessica's Bat Mitzvah date. Bar and Bat Mitzvah students study the Torah and specifically the portion that is to be read on their Bar or Bat Mitzvah date. We originally planned Jessica's Bat Mitzvah the previous year in May and had to cancel because of illness. The new date, a year later, was in April, and the rabbi told us that the same Torah portion as the preceding year was the topic of the evening, even though it was a completely different date on the English calendar. Jessica's Torah portion focused on different ways one can be holy, one of which was showing respect to all people and especially those with disabilities. My speech ended with the following words:

> Jessica, you teach us to be tolerant, loving, and patient. As your Torah portion says, "You teach us to be holy by giving respect and love to those around you."

My parents were not initially supportive of the idea. They questioned whether we should go through all of the trouble and expense. They thought Jessica would be overwhelmed and worried, as we originally did, and that the ceremony might look like a fake or phony Bat Mitzvah. A week after the Bat Mitzvah, we received a beautiful letter from my parents that described how much they learned from this experience.

Dear Vickie and Mitch,

This is a very difficult letter to write. Words alone cannot express the feeling Mother and I had at Jessica's Bat Mitzvah. Sometimes we forget that Jessica, in her way, has the same feelings we all share, and she should also be able to share life's pleasures. When you first told of us of your intentions and that the rabbi was pushing towards having a Bat Mitzvah [Dad's words, not ours], we felt he had his own agenda and was not thinking of you or of Jessica. Well, as last weekend proved, you and the rabbi were right and we were very, very wrong. One of life's greatest rewards is to see your children grow into mature adults, who can make the correct decisions and lead the kind of life that makes one proud to be their parent. The only drawback we felt this weekend was Rita's [Mitch's late mom] absence. She was always so positive and protective of Jessica; she would have been thrilled at the Bat Mitzvah. Again, I have to tell you how proud we are of you…

We love you,
Mother and Dad

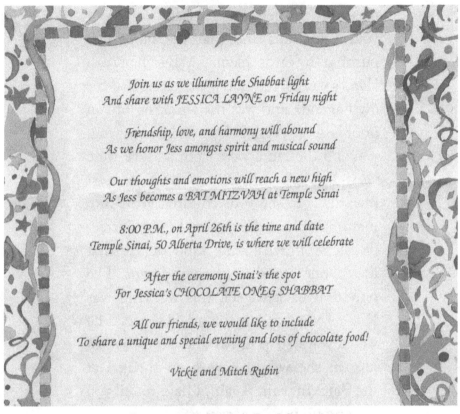

Join us as we illumine the Shabbat light
And share with JESSICA LAYNE on Friday night

Friendship, love, and harmony will abound
As we honor Jess amongst spirit and musical sound

Our thoughts and emotions will reach a new high
As Jess becomes a BAT MITZVAH at Temple Sinai

8:00 P.M., on April 26th is the time and date
Temple Sinai, 50 Alberta Drive, is where we will celebrate

After the ceremony Sinai's the spot
For Jessica's CHOCOLATE ONEG SHABBAT

All our friends, we would like to include
To share a unique and special evening and lots of chocolate food!

Vickie and Mitch Rubin

Invitation to Jessica's Bat Mitzvah.

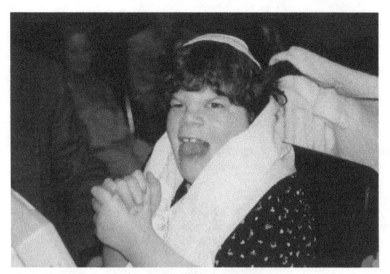

Jessica's Bat Mitzvah Photo.

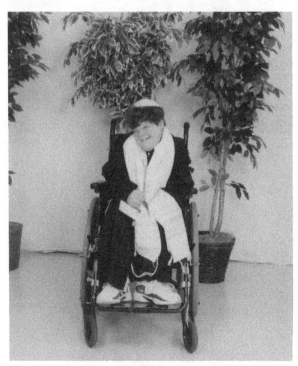

Jessica's Bat Mitzvah Photo.

April 29, 1996

Dear Vickie

This is a very difficult letter to write, words alone can not express the feelings Mother and I had at Jessica's Bat Mitzvah.

Sometimes we forget, that Jessica in her way, has the same feelings we all share, and she should also be able to share life's pleasures. When you first told us of your intentions, and how the Rabbi was pushing you toward having the Bat Mitzvah, we felt he had his own agenda, and was not thinking of you, or of Jessica.

Well as this last Weekend proved, you and the Rabbi were right, and we were very very wrong.

One of life's greatest rewards ,is to see your children grow into mature adults. Adults who can make the correct decisions, and lead the kind of life that makes one proud to be their parent. The only drawback we felt this Weekend was Rita's absence. She was always so positive, and protective of Jessica, she would have been thrilled at the Bat Mitzvah.

Again I have to tell you how proud we are of you, how we admire the way you handle yourself, and the amount of love that you seem to be able to send out in so many directions.

WE LOVE YOU ,

Mith & Dad

Letter from Vickie's parents after
Jessica's Bat Mitzvah.

126

CHAPTER 13

The R-Word

In most homes, a common family rule is not to use swear words. In my childhood home, the use of a swear word directed at somebody was forbidden, but if you were describing a frustrating day or specific situation, it was acceptable to use the F-word in place of darn, dang, or other more civil words. I believe it was my mom who was okay with such language, but I recall that my father's vocabulary was more pristine.

Growing up on Long Island may have desensitized me to the harshness of certain swear words. In my native "New Yawk" tongue, these words were used to emphasize a point. I am not implying that east of Albany the dialect changed or that my family talked like Ozzy Osbourne's family, but in my neck of the woods, it was less of an offense. I quickly learned when I moved to Buffalo that not everyone uses colorful language, so I regretfully toned it down.

As I grew up in the 1960s and '70s, the R-word—*retarded*—was part of everyday vernacular. I know I used the term without thought to the damage and heartache it brought to the person or their family. It was a different era, but that is no excuse, nor is ignorance.

The rules in Mitch's and my home included one word that was off-limits: the R-word. This word has been used loosely in the past. Kids, adults, famous people, and the media used it as if it were an acceptable descriptive expression embraced by the masses. Back in the day, I never heard a bleep on TV when someone said the R-word, and I didn't usually see shock or offense from other listeners. I know this is changing, but there is still more work to be done.

What does the R-word mean to our family? It elicits pain; we feel heartache for Jess, her friends, and our family. This word is different from the curse words described above. In the dictionary, you will find a definition for retarded or mental retardation: "A condition in which a person has an IQ that is below average and that affects an individual's learning, behavior, and development."[14] However, in daily language, it is a slang affront to many individuals who are defenseless and their families.

It's not that people look at Jess and call her names, at least not in front of us. However, when we hear the word so

---

[14] See https://www.merriam-webster.com/dictionary/mental%20retardation. See also https://www.webmd.com/parenting/baby/intellectual-disability-mental-retardation#1

carelessly used, it feels as if they are making fun of Jessica and others with developmental disabilities, even if they are not present to hear the offense. Our beautiful Jess, who brings so much joy and love to the world, should not be referred to in such a mean-spirited, derogatory manner.

Alex and Carly both have clear memories of our perseverance to eliminate this word, at least in our circle of influence. In fact, Carly said that I encouraged them to call out their friends and peers if the word was used in school. Carly often heard the term, but rarely felt comfortable saying anything. Alex told me that he spoke up at school, but that as an adult he no longer admonishes anyone.

Mitch handles the situation a bit differently than me. He corrects people when he hears the R-word and rarely says that the reason he is offended is because he is the father of Jessica. He doesn't want people to think he is extra sensitive. Rather, he wants others to know the word attacks people who often cannot advocate for themselves. He wants people to hear him objectively, not as a father who has been hurt by their comments.

When a child or adult calls another person a retard or says they are acting retarded, they are dehumanizing a population of individuals. This may sound as if I am taking it too far, but if one continues to use the word in casual conversation, he or she becomes desensitized to the word and its meaning that someone is not worthy. It's painful—so painful that a national campaign called Spread the Word to End the Word[15] asks people to pledge not to use the words *retard* or *retarded.*

When Jess was a baby, she was diagnosed with mental retardation based on results of evaluations administered by professionals. It was a clinical term, and as painful as it may be, it was acceptable. When Jess was about five years old, I recall one of her neurologists saying to me, "You know she's retarded." I wish I would have replied with a sarcastic, "I know—thanks for your professional opinion; it is quite helpful." Instead, I nodded and smiled because he was the doctor and I was *only* the parent.

In 2010 President Obama signed a bill replacing the term mental retardation with intellectual disability,[16] and in 2013 the American Psychiatric Association (APA) replaced mental retardation with intellectual developmental disorder.[17] This is a step in the right direction, but we still need to change a culture of people who think the word is acceptable.

When Mitch and I watched political satirist Bill Maher on HBO, he clearly demonstrated that change is still needed. Mr. Maher is politically incorrect, proud of it, and often uses the R-word to describe people in politics to get a laugh from his audience. I became fed up with his antics and searched for a way to contact Mr. Maher to let him know how hurtful his words were in general, and

---

[15] https://specialolympicsri.org/unified-champion-schools/spread-the-word-to-end-the-word/

[16] https://www.disabilityscoop.com/2010/10/05/obama-signs-rosas-law/10547/

[17] August 1, 2013: https://www.federalregister.gov/documents/2013/08/01/2013-18552/change-in-terminology-mental-retardation-to-intellectual-disability

about Jessica in particular. I was unable to find a means of contacting Bill Maher and I almost gave up.

Coincidentally, the University at Buffalo was hosting Bill Maher on April 24, 2010, as part of their Distinguished Speakers Series.[18] One of the components of the Distinguished Speakers Series is the opportunity for the audience to participate in a question-and-answer period after the lecturer completes his or her speech.

Mitch and I bought our tickets, and I had my questions on a folded Post-it note ready to go. The show was particularly painful because Bill Maher focused a lot of his routine on Sarah Palin's son Trig, who has Down syndrome and was two years old at the time. Bill Maher was relentless, and I was building more outrage and courage to speak up. The formal part of the show ended, and I raced up to be first in line for questions. I literally was shaking.

I started by telling Bill Maher that he was very funny, but I wished that he could get the same point across without using the R-word. I added that he was offending many people in the population who were vulnerable and unable to respond to his taunts. Mr. Maher seemed a bit taken aback and asked if my daughter understood his comments. I admitted that she did not, but stated that her mother and family understood his comments. At that point the audience applauded for me, and Bill dismissively moved on to the next questioner.[19]

---

[18] https://www.buffalo.edu/ubreporter/archive/2010_04_28/maher_dss.html

[19] Several weeks later, Mitch was watching Bill Maher on HBO when one of Bill's guests used the R-word. Bill informed the guest that "he [Bill] was told not to use that word anymore."

Unbeknownst to me, our friend Jeremy was sitting in the audience. Jeremy is a bright, articulate, and creative young man who also happens to receive services for his disabilities. Jeremy wrote to Bill Maher and told him that he was in the audience and that he understood the derogatory meaning of the R-word!

In 2017, Mitch and I went to see Bill Maher again, and I am happy to report that he did not use the R-word once at this event. I was waiting for it and was ready to speak up again.

I appeal to my readers that the next time you want to use this word, think of our beautiful Jessica, who is a joy to all who know her. Think of the people who may be hurt by it, and please choose another word.

Jess watching fireworks, July 4, 2015

Jess on a party barge boat, 1990s.

CHAPTER 14

Letting Go

When Jess was young, I had horrible daymares (nightmares while I was awake) about babies left alone in Willowbrook State Institution. If you grew up on Long Island or in the New York Metro area, you knew about Willowbrook.[20]

Willowbrook existed from 1947–1987 and was a place that children with intellectual disabilities were sent to live. In those days these children were classified as mentally retarded or worse descriptors. Conditions at the site were appalling, and it closed in 1987 when federal civil right actions started protecting individuals with disabilities.

---

[20] https://timeline.com/willowbrook-the-institution-that-shocked-a-nation-into-changing-its-laws-c847acb44e0d

In those days, I would lie in bed and think horrific thoughts, vowing to myself that Jess would never go into an institution or group home. Mitch was on the same page as me, although I am not sure that he was going through the same Willowbrook scenarios that ran like a looping video in my mind.

Throughout Jessica's childhood Mitch and I took care of all of Jessica's needs, naïvely thinking that she would never need to move into a group home. As the years progressed and all three of us matured, the necessity of a group home became a reality.

The decision to place one's son or daughter into a group home is monumental. Feelings of guilt, sorrow, relief (yes—there is a bit of relief), uncertainty, and excitement preoccupied our thoughts. We had to face the reality that we were not going to live forever and that finding the right home for Jess would be key to all future planning. Otherwise, what were our options? Did we ask Carly and Alex to take care of Jess? Did we wait until we were so frail that an emergency placement in a random facility is the only remaining option? Didn't Jess have the right to move out of her parents' house and live with peers? Mitch and I needed to consider these issues while we were still clearheaded, and however painful the decision would be, we knew that ultimately getting Jessica into a home in our community—with supports that we wanted in place—was key to both her future and ours.

I think our main fear of letting go was *letting go*. It didn't mean that we would no longer be Jessica's parents, although I was worried that I would not have the same decision-making rights as I did with Jessica at home. Jess could still go to the grocery store with me. We could still be as much a part of Jessica's life as we chose. To this day, we are still her parents; Jess still runs errands with me, we still go to plays, temple, and out to dinner; and most Sundays, Jess comes home for family dinner. Jessica living in a group home also means we are planning for her future when we will not be here to care for her every need.

How does a family take the leap of faith and plan for group home living? For us, it was a gentle stroll toward the inevitable, a slow transition that coincided with our ability to accept the next phase of parenting Jess.

Sometime around 2004, a local rabbi and a temple member, Janet Gunner, initiated the Jewish Group Home (JGH) Committee. Janet has a son with special needs who is much younger than Jess, and she was altruistically initiating this project for other families. (Many years later, Janet would initiate a similar group for her son's home.) I joined our committee in 2004, still thinking the family was not ready for Jessica to move, but hoping to lend my personal and professional expertise in this matter to those who were ready.

Time went on, and Janet asked for a subcommittee of families who were ready to start the first Jewish Group Home together. I joined this group too, but still Mitch and I were not ready, at least we were not ready to *admit* we were ready!

Mitch and I were apprehensive about trusting others to take care of Jessica's daily care. In some ways, it felt like sending our baby to live with others. Jessica was twenty-three but had the life skills of a child. She needed to be continuously watched to make sure that she didn't put foreign objects in her mouth or that other group home residents weren't going to give her food she was unable to chew. We were concerned that staff would be unable to identify some of her more subtle seizures (which still needed to be documented).

Another concern was monitoring Jessica's temperature daily; a spiked fever, if not treated immediately, could lead to more intense seizures. Jessica is unable to tell you when she is ill, and if one didn't read her signs, fever could go undetected, often resulting in a trip to the emergency room.

Mitch and I talked about alternatives to group home living and realized that moving Jessica while we were still young enough to be a constant presence in her new home was the right decision. All our fears listed above would not go away if we waited another ten years. However, Jessica's opportunity to live in a household that was going to be part of our Jewish community, side by side with families we were comfortable with and within two miles from our residence, was not going to happen again. We realized we had to say yes. We started visiting existing group homes and talking to staff and families so that we could grow more comfortable with Jessica's next home. Eventually, Mitch and I were ready for our family to take the next step.

In May of 2006, the first Jewish Women's Group Home was on the way to being built. We had five Jewish women, of which Jessica was one, who would move into their new home. We were ready for Jessica and our family to make this life-changing transition.

Our Jewish Women's Group Home subcommittee, led by Janet, met for approximately two years and became each other's extended family. We felt confident that each of us would also watch over the four other women in the house. I believe the time it took to bond and trust our fellow group home members helped ease our transition to a new reality.

We worked with the largest human service agency in our region, People Inc. We chose them because we believed they had the experience and knowledge about building group homes and would be flexible to meet our needs and respect our daughters Jewish tradition and culture.

Janet and Temple Beth Tzedek (TBZ) were an integral part of the process. We were invited to holiday services at TBZ where the future residents had additional opportunities to socialize and get to know each other. Janet and the rabbi attended every subcommittee meeting; Janet, an attorney, offered her expertise of the law, and the rabbi shared insightful words of wisdom to us and guidance to People Inc. about Jewish living.

The following excerpts are taken from a column I wrote for our local newspaper in May of 2007 and illustrate some of the feelings we had to work through at the time.

Jess is moving in two months.

Monday to Friday morning...6 a.m., roll out of bed, make lunch for our daughter, change her undergarments, dress her for the day, feed her breakfast, juice, vitamins, medications, comb hair, brush teeth, and send her off to school by 7 a.m. Total care, assistance with all daily life skills—that is what Mitch and I did—we cared for Jess and assisted with every task that one needs for daily living, similar to the care of an infant or toddler. At twenty-five, Jessica was moving into her own home. Hard as this may be to believe, in many respects, we were going to miss the daily care.

Today I changed all of Jessica's winter clothes, put them in boxes, brought out the summer clothing, and put them in Jessica's drawers. The reality was, I wouldn't be doing this anymore. She will have "staff," assistants who will provide the tasks of daily life. They will dress and feed Jessica, administer medications, and take care of her daily needs. And we will miss this too.

We will long for the constant humming in our house; Jess can hum about twenty-five tunes (and counting). No matter how gloomy the day, we have constant "Muzak" in our home. We will miss the persistent grabs for a hug, the cheek turned towards us, gesturing a kiss, her hands reaching for a dog and, her constant smile and good cheer.

What will I do for dinner every night? For twenty-five years I have been feeding both Jess and me at the same time. I've gotten pretty good at it; now where will that skill go? My husband and I joke that nobody can change a diaper faster than us—we have twenty-five years of practice. I don't know where or when the challenge would ever come up, but I am sure we would win [a competition], and yes, we will miss that, too.

I have a monitor in our room; I listen and hear everything in Jessica's room every night. Now I will only be listening to the loud snoring beside me. Do I still need the intercom? I guess not; in fact, now I may feel comfortable wearing ear plugs to eradicate the snoring. Previously, I didn't dare muffle any potential unusual sounds from the monitor. This leads me to think that my husband and I are always on call, even when sleeping, and that will change too. What will we do with that energy? Hmmm…

I think we are well known in our neighborhood; we are the family with three dogs and one young singing lady in a wheelchair, and we walk—we walk a lot—and I will miss that, as well.

I go to every doctor appointment, dentist appointment, neurologist, endocrinologist, primary care physician, ear, nose and throat specialist, and physiatrist. (Definition: a physician who specializes in physical medicine and rehabilitation; who knew there was such a field?) Will I continue to go to these appointments? I was told that many families do not attend routine appointments; instead they receive a follow-up call. Will I become the follow-up call or continue to go to every appointment? Most likely, I will continue to actively participate with her physicians. I like talking to the doctors, I need to know what is going on, and I will miss the fact that she can now go to an appointment regardless of my schedule.

Jess is moving into a group home this summer; she's twenty-five and it's time. Time for Jess to learn how to live as an adult woman who needs assistance. Time for my husband and me to begin to let go of the physical daily care.

The group home is less than two miles from our home. We will be close, we will still be her guardians, still a presence in her daily life, still her loving parents, still on-call yet; there will be enormous changes, many of which we haven't even thought of yet.

The other day I went to visit the house, which is almost complete, and was given Jessica's phone number. It was a peculiar feeling to enter Jessica's number into my cell phone; she will not share our phone number for the first time. I never thought about Jessica having her own phone number.

Our other two children are now young adults, living in [college] dorms. We always anticipated, embraced, and expected their independence. We knew that if we did our job well, they would be able to live independently. We did not allow ourselves, until a few years ago, to consider that Jess was going to move as well. Was it denial? What were we thinking? Was it possible that we would be able to provide daily care forever? No, none of the above. It was just hard to accept that there would be a point when it was time to let Jess move in with her peers, enjoy her own level of independence, and have her own phone number.

Recently we celebrated Mother's Day, and maybe that is why I am thinking about all the ways my mothering will be different, or maybe it's just getting close to moving date and reality is setting in; things will be changing, and in many ways, we will miss our old life.

I wrote the above before Jessica moved into her new home and didn't know how life would change from that point. It took a while for me to find myself; I had identified myself as a mom who had a 24/7 responsibility. Who was I now? Who were Mitch and I as a couple? We needed to find out.

---

https://www.people-inc.org/

Family photo in front of Jessicas home.

Jessica in her stander playing mini
piano at group home.

CHAPTER 15

Getting by with a Little Help from My Friends

As soon as we started to let go, tragedy struck in Jessica's new home. Within the first three months of the house opening, one of the young women unexpectedly passed away. She was the youngest person in the house—a bright, joyful woman and a delight to be around. She was vibrant, which made her death even more shocking.

We were all devastated. Our families had worked together to put every detail in place for close to four years; we were one another's extended family and the sorrow was palpable.

The night that her housemate passed, we took Jessica back to our home to stay with us. We were struggling with our next step. Should we keep Jessica with us and restart the group home process ten years later? We didn't know how to make that decision.

The next day we heard a few specifics about how the house staff had worked diligently to save Jess's friend's life and that her medical condition may have been the cause of death. Mitch and I brought Jess back to the house a day later. We remained extremely vigilant over the next few months until we once again felt comfortable with the care at the house.

The bedroom of our deceased loved one remained vacant for close to one year. I believe People Inc.'s administration was giving us time to fully grieve.

One day late in 2007, I heard a rumor that a young woman may be moving into the house.

I think everyone was ready to open the door to a new friend. Lizzy moved into the house and immediately lit the place up with her sparkling energy. She quickly charmed Jess and Karen and found creative ways to communicate with both women who are non-verbal. Lizzy is a social superstar, and her enthusiasm and gregarious nature spread joy to all the women. She was just what everyone needed!

Five years later, Jessica had a frightening incident herself, and I credit our son Alex for saving her life. Below is a portion of an email which I wrote on November 6, 2012, describing the event.

> Jess went to the hospital by ambulance this evening. Jess, Mitch and I are home from the hospital now. A higher power was in our world this evening. Alex went to visit Jess and said that Jess wasn't right, she was coughing and looked "off." Staff at the house didn't appear to be as concerned; they thought it may be sudden congestion(?). Alex called me at work. Mitch also drove to the house.
>
> When I got there, I knew Jess was choking and called 911. Her pulse ox [blood oxygen] was good, but her eyes were watering and bulging. And she had thrown up a few times. When we got to the ER, she threw up—and a friggen' red potato, fully intact, came out! It looked, at first, as if she expelled an organ! I and medical staff didn't know what it was.
>
> Now we must figure out how it happened and make sure it won't happen again. I know that thousands of meals have been given without incident. But I am concerned that the trend of care at the house may not be at the same level. Tonight was very scary and could have

gone in another awful direction. Jess is now back to her singing self. Thankfully.

We never found out how a small red potato ended up in Jessica's food, and ultimately her throat. Jessica is on a soft diet, with her food ground in a food processor like a infant's meal. After the incident, new protocols were installed and food preparation monitoring put in place. This episode demonstrates how much we rely on family, friends, and observant staff to keep Jessica from harm. All that can go wrong is daunting, and if we dwell on it too much, we can drive ourselves nuts.

Group home life is not seamless—not even close. The staff pay is very low, and the work is exhausting and frequently unpleasant. Mitch and I need to remain vigilant to ensure that Jessica's needs are met. There are a multitude of details that *can* go wrong, *do* go wrong, and *will* go wrong. There are also numerous moments that can only be described as beautiful and unexpected because many staff and friends have gone far beyond any of our expectations.

Jessica's current house manager, Kelly, is so wonderful that I am thankful for her every day. She has a nursing background, treats the women as her family members, lives a mile from the group home, and is a tremendous advocate. I can call or text Kelly whenever there is a concern. I feel calmer when she is there.

Throughout the past twelve years, we have been blessed with staff at the group home who have risen above the rest and have become family to us. Their titles vary from service coordinator, manager, and personal care aides to the multitude of other staff that make life possible at Jessica's home. There are so many who have made a mark on our Jessica and our family that I cannot name them all in this book, but I hope that they know the difference they have made in our lives.

Some people work with our daughter because they feel a calling. Others choose this field because they have a friend or relative with a disability and they developed an interest in helping others. Many have an intrinsic need to make a difference in another person's life. There are amazing people who walk through Jessica's doors, and we appreciate them every day.

On the other hand, there are also staff who make you cringe—the ones with their faces in their phones or who are watching TV while the women are unattended; the ones who don't smile, the ones who don't care, and the ones who don't show up, so others need to work double shifts. This field of work has a poor retention rate, and it feels like a revolving door of new people. I try to learn names, but by the time I do, they are no longer employed. The pay scale is so low that finding career-minded staff is a struggle when they could make higher wages at a fast-food restaurant. The personal care, patience, and responsibility required of this position far outweighs the salary. There is an advocacy group in New York working to increase salary to a living wage for those who are entrusted with the lives of individuals with developmental disabilities. Their tag line is #BeFair2DirectCare (website: bfair2directcare.com).

It has been twelve years since Jessica moved into her home. Currently, she participates in community activities, goes bowling with her house, and celebrates birthdays and holidays with her housemates. She lives with her friends and shares their joys and heartaches.

Last week, one of her friends asked if she could come to our house for dinner with Jessica. We were thrilled that she has a friend who does not need Jessica to speak words for communication to take place. This friend also has learned a lot from Jessica. To add some confusion to the following story, her housemate's name is also Jessica. I will refer to her as JT.

JT told her mother that she would "like to be happy like Jessica." JT's mom replied, "Being happy is a choice and you can choose to feel happy." That night, JT and her mom went out to dinner, and JT started humming a familiar tune. Her mom asked JT what she was doing, and she replied, "I am trying to feel happiness like Jess." This story highlights that fact that everyone has something to learn and everyone can be a teacher and a friend. We all want our adult children to have friends, and it is no different for Jessica. She has made true friends in her home.

Jessica also has two local friends whom she shares with me and our family. These two woman, Sheryl and Ellen, have ensured that Jessica's group home life is full.

Ellen, Sheryl, and I are family by choice, not by blood. We affectionately call one another sisters.

Ellen and Sheryl were always close with Jessica, so it was not a surprise that when Jess moved into her new home, they remained part of her inner circle. They have embraced Jessica as their family member and visit her regardless if

Mitch or I are there; they make the effort and they visit because they love Jess.

They have also become close with the five ladies who reside together. In fact, one of Jessica's housemates will constantly ask where Sheryl is when I visit. Sheryl comes in like a bolt of lightning, and all the women are immediately engaged. She sings, tells jokes, gives great hugs, and is truly interested in the women.

I originally knew Sheryl from the Jewish community only to give a wave and a brief hello. But then Sheryl moved next door to us. Her first words could have ended the friendship immediately when she looked at her new home, so much larger than ours, and said to me, "I am downsizing." I didn't know it at the time, but Sheryl and her family were having financial problems and had to leave their beautiful newly built home and truly downsize. All I thought at the time was, *That's rude. Your house is so much bigger than mine!*

Soon after, Mitch and I bought a wooden swing for our front yard where Jess and I could swing and watch Carly and Alex play. Sheryl started walking over when we were outside and began sitting next to Jess. Eventually, it became 5:00 p.m. somewhere, and Sheryl and I would sip a glass of wine. This became the beginning of our friendship and the rest, as they say, is history.

Ellen is a bit more reserved, but has the same dedication to Jess. I met Ellen when our kids were in preschool. We quickly became friends, and through the years, our friendship has grown into the aforementioned sisterhood. Ellen's career was in the disability field, and she attends all of Jessica's meetings as both friend and advocate. I don't ask Ellen to attend; she asks me when and where Jessica's next meeting is.

I am not sure how it happened that we were blessed with Sheryl and Ellen's friendship. Adversity in one's life also opens doors to seeing the capacity of others to care. I know Jessica has something to do with it because her reaction when she sees people that she deeply loves is off the charts. Without speaking a word, her face beams and she screams and jumps up and down in her wheelchair. There have been times that I thought her wheelchair would tip over backward.

Mitch and I will never become snowbirds in Florida or move away from the Buffalo, New York, region. And even though Jess lives in a group home, she is still our daughter and needs intense family involvement. It is crucial to Jessica's well-being that there are others besides Mitch and I who care and visit.

When Sheryl first moved next door to us, her car broke down. Sheryl's parents were visiting from Brooklyn, and I was in New York visiting my parents. My van was resting comfortably in the driveway, so Mitch walked over to Sheryl, introduced himself, and offered her my van while I was away. As Mitch walked back home, Sheryl's father, Phil, said, "You just moved next door to an angel!" In my opinion, on that date, an angel moved next door to us.

Jess and Ellen.

Jess and Sheryl, 2017.

Jess, Ellen, and Sheryl.

Sheryl, Ellen, Barb, and Jess.

Jess and housemate Karen in their home.

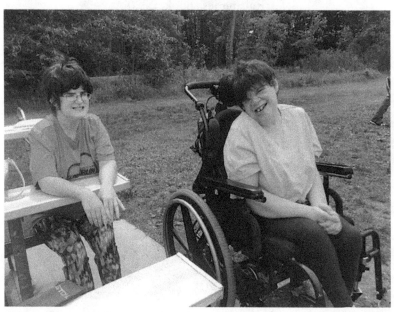

Jess and housemate Jessica T.

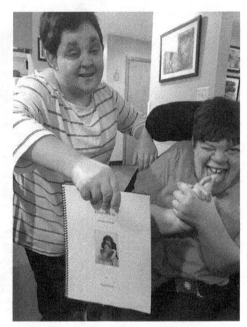

Jess and Liz holding prototype of
Raising Jess book, 2020

Joe and his daughter Karen enjoying the
group home's baseball team, 2008.

Liz, her mom Cathy, and Karen on
the porch of the group home.

CHAPTER 16

The Gift of Grandparents

Raising Jess was not just about our nuclear family of five; her birth greatly affected her grandparents. At the time of this writing, Jess is thirty-seven years old. Mitch's beloved mom Rita passed away in 1992, and his dad Marty has been remarried to Norma for twenty-six years. My mother Dianne has Alzheimer's, and my dad Monroe originally took on the role of her full-time caretaker. But at eighty-eight, this has become physically impossible. They now have two remarkable aides who come to their house, around the clock, to support my mom.

I wish I would have thought of interviewing my parents prior to 2019.

My parents now live in Florida, as do most of their Long Island friends. Monroe was a successful owner of a dress manufacturing company in the New York City garment center. He was a strict disciplinarian while I was growing up, and I tested him often. Even though I consistently lost our battles, I did not give up my quest for independence and too much fun. Mom did not need to be as strict because she had Dad, and her usual 1970s retort was, "Wait till your father gets home!"

My mom's and my relationship morphed into a beautiful adult friendship once I had children. Mom and I used to talk on the phone daily for close to thirty-six years until her illness progressed and communication over the phone became difficult. My dad and I now talk on the phone every day, whereas in the past he would give a warm hello and say, "Here's your mom." We chat about all kinds of things from politics to books and, of course, my mom. As devastating as Mom's illness is to her and our family, it has deepened the connection and friendship that I have with my father.

Recently, I wanted to open a dialogue about Jessica's grandparents' perspective and sent my initial email to Dad. I informed him that I was interviewing everyone about their relationship with Jess and emailed the questions in the hope that it would be easier for him to ponder at his own pace.

Dad's reply was the following:

> Tough questions. I am thinking about it
> and realized I came up short as a grand-
> father. Questions have made me go back
> and think. I would prefer to do this face-
> to-face when you come down to Florida.
> In general, I treated Jess more like an
> object. I loved her and only wanted the
> best for her. I know I would do anything
> to make her life easier, but the interaction
> was different. It opened up a lot of ques-
> tions. I am afraid I came up short.

I was daunted after I received Dad's answer to my
interview. "I think I came up short" resonated with me. I
did not expect that response, and although in many ways
he and my mom did come up short, they also provided
other types of support that made our life livable.

My answer to him said:

> I will do a face-to-face interview. The
> questions were not intended to hurt you—
> your help made the difference between
> us making it and not, so if you think you
> came up short in one area, you exceeded
> in others.

And his response was the following:

> I know that, but it started me thinking.
> At the time I did not think we were doing
> anything wrong. My problem is hind-
> sight—makes you think.

I truly appreciated his honesty and tried to make sense of his words. My dad was born in 1930 and raised in an extremely different era where individuals with disabilities were rarely cared for at home. There has been an evolution of societal attitudes toward disability, but I had to consider the time period in which my father was brought up and what the norms were for parents of that period. Back in the day, it would have been unusual for a child with a disability to be visible; most spent their childhood in institutions and were seldom seen in public.

One exception to the above is the story of our friend Joe and his late wife Rena. Joe is the same age as my dad and his daughter Karen lives in the group home with Jess. Joe has a PhD in biochemistry and is a former professor at the State University at Buffalo. His wife Rena was also incredibly bright and an extraordinary advocate for Karen. Joe and Rena were raised in the same era as my parents. Their daughter Karen was born in 1964 with cerebral palsy and needs assistance with all daily life skills.

Joe often talks about the era in which Karen was born. He says, "There were no supports; we were on our own." Joe and Rena nurtured Karen in their household until she was five, and then she moved into a residential center close to their home; group homes did not exist at that time. They did not have the Early Intervention Program or any respite other than family members. The unique thing about Joe and Rena is that they remained as involved in Karen's life as if she were living with them. She slept home on weekends and was included in all family events and celebrations when she was growing up.

I met Joe and Rena when we were creating the group home for our daughters. The year was 2005, and their involvement was equal to the families whose children still lived with their parents. Joe never moved from Buffalo; his two other sons live quite a distance away, but his and Rena's dedication to Karen included remaining in Western New York—even in the winter. When Karen was born, moving her to an institution was encouraged and expected because of limited services to help families nurture their child in their home and the stigma of raising a child with a disability. I think Joe and Rena did the best they could with the inadequate community support at the time.

I sometimes wonder how my parents would have handled having a daughter like Jessica in the late-1950s. My parents' experience with individuals with disabilities was limited, and their views were created by the attitudes of society in the decades they were raised. I don't blame them for not knowing how to get involved. Perhaps I should have made suggestions or encouraged more interaction, but I also didn't know how to do that.

My parents were extremely generous financially, and their support in that way made a significant difference in our life. Their assistance was crucial for us to be able to raise Jessica without sinking.

When I asked Dad what he would have changed, he replied, "I would have spent more time with you." Dad also said that he was concerned about our marriage and the amount of work that fell on me. He was troubled that we were raising Jess at home.

I read a study on the effect on having a grandchild with disabilities on grandparents, which states that grandparents experience what is termed "double grief" because they are grieving both for their grandchild and their children.[21] In hindsight, I realize I was so wrapped up in my experience that it never occurred to me to ask what my parents or in-laws were feeling. Now that Mitch and I are grandparents, we have better understanding of the depth of pain our parents experienced.

I believe Mom couldn't get past what she envisioned as her daughter's hardship to see the delightful, beautiful granddaughter who was our joy. On the other hand, Mom appreciated the passion I had for my role and constantly said, "You should write a book." I always took offense to this suggestion because I had a career, I was helping others, I was in charge. It felt as if she was dismissing what I was doing. In retrospect, it feels as if she saw in me what I did not recognize in myself. Unfortunately, once I started

---

[21] Sandra Woodbridge, Laurie Buys, and Evonne Miller, "Grandparenting a Child with a Disability: An Emotional Rollercoaster," Australasian Journal on Ageing, 28, no. 1 (2009): pp. 37–40. The study is available to download at https://core.ac.uk/download/pdf/10894041.pdf.

writing this book, it coincided with Mom's failing memory and health.

I tried to interview my mother, who at eighty-four has a limited vocabulary because of Alzheimer's. When I asked how she felt about being a parent of an adult facing a life-altering diagnosis for their child, she replied in her now halted speech, "Felt terrible. Never felt better about it." One thing to know about growing up with my mom is she had very few filters and you could always count on her to be honest. The Alzheimer's has removed whatever filters she did have, and Mom was completely honest with what she was able to say. I believe she missed out on what could have been a beautiful relationship with Jess, but I do not blame her for loving me so much that she couldn't get past her devastation.

My in-laws moved from the Bronx in New York to Buffalo in 1963. Mitch's dad Marty was entrepreneurial and chose Buffalo as a location to open a check-cashing business. He also owned a successful wholesale watch business.

Mitch's mom Rita was a gifted teacher and I still get comments from peers about how her teaching changed their life. She passed away in 1992, way too early, and is lovingly remembered, not only by family and friends, but also by her students. Rita was very warm and loving with Jessica. She was a tremendous support for Jess and our family. And not only was she my mother-in-law, she was my friend. We feel her absence and it grieves us to think about all that she missed.

Marty married Norma in 1993, and they have been married for twenty-six years. Jess and Norma have a friendly, loving relationship. There are plenty of smiles when Jess sees Norma. But truly, nobody would deny the way that Jess lights up when she sees Marty in person. He has always had her heart.

I emailed my in-laws the same questions that I sent to Dad. Norma replied with a thoughtful note that described her impressions about our family.

> I will try to share my thoughts, things I think about often when I think about you, Mitch, and Jess, along with Alex and Carly.
>
> I have often thought that Mitch and you were incredibly brave to have more children. It had to take a lot of courage, and a big leap of faith and it paid off with the beautiful, healthy, wonderful children that followed. I know people who were in a similar situation and were unwilling to take the risk.
>
> And I also always admire how much joy your family and Jess share. She is such a happy person, music in her soul, and seems to be content with herself and her life, and at the same time has brought so much joy to others. You and Mitch have played a large part in helping her develop in such a lovely way.

I also admire that you chose a career that not only was of personal interest to you, but also helped so many other people in similar situations.

Hope this helps,
Love, Norma

Marty was straightforward in his reply. His reaction to learning about Jessica was "sadness for both of you. It was devastating to learn your son's first-born child was born severely handicapped. Devastating to Rita and me."

He said he later learned to accept the diagnosis. I recall prior to Jessica's first visit with a specialist in New York that Marty was adamant that Jessica was fine and did not need all those evaluations. Denial? Perhaps. Or maybe he truly felt that way.

When I asked what he saw as his role as a grandparent, he replied, "To do what I could when asked and that his role was no different than with our other kids except a far greater social and physical interaction with them."

When I inquired if he would have changed anything, his reply was, "Looking back, I believe I would not have done anything different."

Our thoughts were how can you do it physically, as well as not creating a family environment filled with extreme tensions among you all. Our greater concerns were not with Jess, but with Alex and Carly.

Jess was getting the attention. I have to say, though, you both did a tremendous job in juggling the needs and dynamics within the family.

Jessica's face lights up whenever she sees Marty. No matter how long they have been apart, she is thrilled to see him in person and on Facetime. Marty and Jessica share the love of the song, "Too-Ra-Loo-Ra-Loo-Ral (That's an Irish Lullaby)"; however, Marty modifies his version with "that's a Jewish lullaby," adding to their mutual delight.

Finally, I asked Marty what his favorite memory of Jess was and he replied, "Her ever-smiling face and her inner happiness." Marty believes that he "is more sensitive to the handicapped," as he puts it.

We were blessed, as mentioned in a previous chapter, with Great-grandma Rose, who was born in the early 1900s. Presumably, Rose had less experience with individuals with disabilities than any of Jessica's grandparents, yet she seemed to embrace Jessica, her *zis meydl* (Yiddish phrase for sweet girl) as if there were no differences.

If Jessica could speak, I believe she would agree with much of the above. Jess gets to see my parents once or twice a year, but that doesn't hinder her reaction when they visit. When she sees her grandparents, she will scream and hyperventilate and try to jump from her seat. So although Jess can't say the words "I love you" or "I am so happy to see you," she lets you know. Jess has the ability to show her love and not judge; she ignores the baggage and embraces the positive. That is the gift Jessica gives her grandparents.

Grandpa Marty, Grandma Norma,
Jess, Alex, and Carly, 1990s

Great-grandma Dianne and Brady, 2019.

Jess and paternal Grandpa Marty.

Jessica's late paternal grandmother, Rita.

Mitch, Alex, Steve, Carly, Vickie, Grandma
Norma, Grandpa Marty, and Jess.

Mitch and our friend Dr. Joe Merrick—
daughter Karen lives with Jess.

Mitch's father, Marty—Jess, Alex, and Carly.

Mitch's mother Rita and father Marty with Jess, 1983.

Paternal Great-grandma Rose with Jessica.

Paternal Great-grandparents Sam and Bella.

Jessica's Grandpa Monroe, Vickie's father.

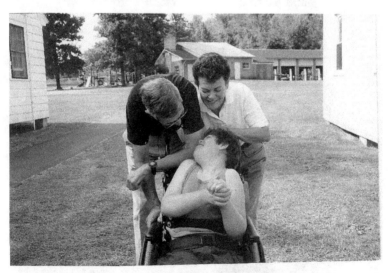

Jessica with Grandpa Monroe and Grandma
Dianne, maternal grandparents.

From Left: Mitch, Leo and Sayde Schlanger
(Vickie's grandparents), Monroe Schlanger
holding Jessica, Vickie, Dianne Schlanger
and Keith Schlanger (Vickie's brother)

Karen and dad Joe at group home.

CHAPTER 17

She's My Sister

This is the chapter that is supposed to describe the perceived trauma, despair, and life-altering results of growing up with Jess, as told by Jessica's siblings, Alex and Carly.

I struggled with all the unknowns in this section. First off, did I want to hear how we may have ruined Jessica's siblings' lives? Who really wants to know all the mistakes made while raising siblings of children with disabilities? I researched other sibling stories and learned about families who insisted that their siblings become caretakers of their brother or sister with a disability after the parents are no longer on this planet.[22]

The articles described some siblings who felt they were neglected because their brother or sister needed so much attention. Other siblings were concerned about catching the disability. I read one story of a young girl who had a history of amazing grades in school, but one year, she faced difficulties and did not receive As on her report card. Her first thought was that she was catching her sister's intellectual disability. She never told her parents about her fear because she didn't want to upset them.

So when it came to interviewing Jessica's brother and sister, I was a bit apprehensive of the negativity that could be revealed. Was I ready to hear things that I couldn't unhear or unknow? The answer was yes, I was ready—kind of.

In hindsight, I believe that having these interviews was worth the entire process of writing the story of our journey of raising Jess. I would recommend this to parents of adult children. It's like an exit survey when you leave a corporation. The human resource personnel will ask about your experience at their company. "So how did we do? Any improvements we can make? Where did we come up short, and where did we excel?" Although there really isn't a chance for improvement because they are grown, it was an amazing opportunity for reflection and thoughtful conversation.

---

[22] Mortality is another topic that parents of individuals with disabilities need to face a bit more than their peers. Mitch and I are always talking about what will happen when we can't be there for Jess—but we are really asking what will happen when we are dead.

This chapter has been the most difficult to write of any section in this book because of my fears about what I might uncover. When I told my daughter, Carly, about my frustration, she said, "Mom, maybe there isn't enough difference that we felt to add a chapter because Alex and I don't believe that our life growing up was unlike that of our friends." That's quite a statement, and if it's true, Mitch and I did something right.

Life was different for us, but somehow we juggled it well. This was not with well-thought-out planning or strategic scheduling or even "brainwashing" our kids to believe that things *were normal*. We simply had the philosophy that we were not going to be limited.

Mitch and I appreciate that the kids believe it wasn't *that* different, but after rereading their interviews, I have some thoughts that may highlight some of the uniqueness of their childhood.

Alex and Carly are dissimilar from each other in personality, organization, recreational styles, appearance—you get the picture—they are not alike, yet they both feel very connected to Jess in their unique way.

Carly, in 2019, is thirty-two and Alex is thirty-five. They are both married and have given us amazing grandchildren (Nana bias permitted). Alex received his master's in sports management and dreamed of working in the front office of a national sports team, if not in Buffalo, in another state. But then Joyce came into his life and said staying in Buffalo was nonnegotiable. Joyce was way more appealing than the front office, so Buffalo became their home. I always say that if I had created a job description for the woman that Alex would marry, Joyce would have exceeded every point on the list. Joyce has her master's in special education, is so funny that I am constantly laughing at her dry humor, and is beautiful to look at; but more importantly, she's beautiful inside her self-described "old soul." As Alex states in his interview, "I had to marry somebody who not only accepts Jessica but embraces Jessica." He scored!

Carly met her husband Steve in undergraduate school. They endured many years apart while she pursued her doctorate in physical therapy by traveling back and forth from Oswego, New York, to Buffalo and eventually from New Haven, Connecticut, to Buffalo. To say they were committed is an understatement. I became a fan of Steve very early in their relationship. It was Christmas Eve and as I mentioned, our Jewish family always had a party in New York on Christmas Day. Mitch and I drove to Steve's parents' house near Oswego to pick up Carly and continue our trip to Long Island. Carly was quite ornery on this trip (which is not always a red flag), but when we got to our hotel, we realized that she was sick. Eventually we found out she had mononucleosis, but we didn't know that right away. The only thing that made Carly smile during this illness was phone calls (and there were a lot) from her new boyfriend, Steve. How can a mother not love to see her baby smiling amid mono-misery? When we finally came back to Buffalo, Steve visited and was so attentive. Not only did he seal the deal with Carly, but Mitch and I were onboard too.

Mitch and I feel blessed that Carly and Alex chose life partners that we embrace as our family and love deeply and that both son-in-law and daughter-in-law treat Jess with love, kindness, and acceptance. I have heard about potential suitors who are alarmed when they see that their significant other's sibling has a severe disability and fear that it could happen to their family, thus ending the relationship.

Let's go back a bit to the years growing up with Jess.

Carly and Alex both went to the same high school, although they were three grades apart. Alex was in the chorus plus every musical play, and Carly played violin in the orchestra. Mitch, Jess, and I were huge fans and attended all performances. It took only a moment for everyone to know our family. Jess was typically the only person in a large wheelchair; if there were other wheelchairs, it was usually a travel chair for an elderly relative. As soon as we rolled into the auditorium, Jess would scream with glee. Everyone knew us; whether they were happy to see us is another story.

Jess was happy to be at the high school performances, and she showed it the only way she knew how—by humming, clapping, screeching, and making herself known. I often whispered into her ear to distract her; unfortunately, it also distracted me from watching the stage. This was a constant dilemma to us. On one hand, Jess is a family member and loved going to the concerts and we wanted her there, but on the other hand, the energy it took to get her there and keep her joy to a low decibel was exhausting. Carly and Alex both told me they were never embarrassed about Jessica's disability, yet they both, independently, spoke about cringing at the loud hums and sounds that

Jessica emitted at public venues, specifically their high school performances and at temple.

Another topic was family vacations. It's a good thing Alex and Carly weren't asked to give testimony in court because Alex said we went on many trips while Carly thought our vacations were limited. We did not go on trips like some of our friends; we didn't stay in resorts nor fly off to far-off islands. In fact, as I mentioned in chapter 8, Mitch and I eventually decided to divide and conquer; Mitch or I would travel with Carly or Alex separately, while the other parent stayed home with Jess. This provided a bit more freedom to explore without all the stress.

I remember one ambitious family vacation. Mitch and I awoke the kids at 11:00 p.m. and drove to Florida. Jess was ten, Alex seven, and Carly was turning five that week. This was the first and last time we drove with all the kids to Florida. It was before we had our wheelchair van and the three kids sat in the back. Jess was the only one who did not fall asleep once during our twenty-four-hour drive. Jess spent the hours grabbing and pinching her siblings, and as you can guess, it was only fun for her. Thinking back, how were Alex and Carly supposed to react to that? They couldn't and wouldn't retaliate, but nevertheless, it was extremely annoying and sometimes painful. Oddly, neither of them brought this up in our interview.

Our vacation started with a visit to my parents in southern Florida and ended with a trip to Disney World on Carly's birthday. It was a truly magical trip. Twenty-seven years later, Mitch and I still talk about the royal treatment we received at Disney World because of Jessica. There are some perks to having a wheelchair, and Disney World is one place that rolls out the red carpet. We were put first in line for every attraction Jessica could experience, and we were led through back doors to limit waiting and sun exposure. Through all the years, it is still one of the best experiences we have had in a public venue. When I asked Carly and Alex about family vacations, neither spoke about this trip to Florida.

When talking with Carly about her childhood, she admitted that she always felt like the oldest even though she was the youngest (we felt that way too). Her perspective was that she had to use an alarm to wake up and make her own breakfast and lunch for school. She mentioned that if she forgot something at school, we did not bring it in for her, but she wasn't sure if that was discipline or because of Jessica. She said that she rarely forgot things but that Alex often left homework at home, and perhaps if Jess hadn't need so much assistance in the morning, we could have focused more on Alex's needs for organization. Carly feels as if she missed out on a sister-sister relationship; in fact, she still feels that Jess doesn't get very excited to see her. She added that there was no sister role model; as a kid she didn't get along with Alex and felt she missed the potential for a better sibling experience.

When the kids were in middle school, each afternoon we had a personal care aide for Jess in the house (if they showed up). I remember one scary time that an aide was unable to come because of extreme weather and Alex and Carly were completely responsible for Jess while an unexpected blizzard was accelerating in Buffalo.

It was November 2000, and I was about twenty minutes away from our home, taking a work seminar on creating PowerPoint trainings. It was all the rage back then, and I was eager to learn how to master this program. We had small windows in the classroom, and it snowed all day, but nobody was particularly concerned. The class ended at 3:00 p.m. and I went to my car planning to be home before 3:30 and Jessica's bus. That was an optimistic plan. Once I saw the road conditions, I knew it was going to be a long haul. I opened my flip phone to call Mitch, and he was in the same predicament but in the opposite direction. We later found out that most people realized at 3:00 p.m. they needed to get home as soon as possible because of the weather, which created huge traffic jams.

The National Weather Service website for western New York weather history describes the storm as follows:

> Snow fell at the rate of two to four inches per hour for several hours. The storm crippled much of the Buffalo metro area. Tens of thousands of people were stranded in autos as city and suburban streets became clogged with traffic and came to a standstill. Three thousand school children were [stranded] in buses which were unable to complete their routes. Snowfall in this early stage [was] as high as two feet in a narrow strip about three miles wide.[23]

---

[23] https://www.weather.gov/buf/HistoryNov22.html

Meanwhile, Carly and Alex were home from school, the aide had cancelled, and Jess was due home momentarily. My car crept along the roads as I tried to navigate the route; whiteouts blinded me and the other drivers' vision, but we were hearty Buffalonians and we crept along. I called the kids often to see if Jess got home and how they were faring. I think most parents would be worried that their teens were home alone during a blizzard, but that was pushed aside as we not only worried about them but had the added stress of them managing Jessica's care.

A flurry of questions whirled through our minds like the falling snow. What if Mitch and I were both stranded? We have heard of this happening repeatedly during blizzards. Would they manage? What if the electricity went out? Or the heat? What if Jess had a seizure? Could they change her diapers and keep her comfortable? How would they feel about this responsibility? How would the kids take care of Jess all night long? What about dinner? Additional meds? Alex was sixteen and Carly thirteen; was this too much pressure to put on them? (As a side note to parents who think their kids will be scarred for life by certain events, Alex did not remember this incident or the snowstorm.)

Jessica's bus eventually made it to our home. Thankfully, she was the last person dropped off at her residence before the busses had to stop driving and return all other passengers to a central location. Many of the students on the bus needed seizure and other crucial medications. Parents were unable to reach their children because of the roads, and there was a feeling of alarm. I later read about families walking miles in the blizzard carrying medicine and clothing for their children.

Meanwhile, Alex and Carly got Jess off the bus and set about keeping her routine. They gave her juice, snacks, and afternoon seizure medication. We called often and said, "We are almost home," but it was slow going. Alex and Carly (maybe more Carly since Alex has no memory of the event) kept the routine going, took care of Jess, and most importantly, didn't panic as Mitch and I continued to drive separately and desperately to reach home.

Mitch and I were so proud that Carly and Alex handled the unexpected emergency with calmness, expertise, and good nature—at least that's how I remember it. Mitch and I arrived home safely. It took each of us more than three hours to travel the twenty-minute route. Our teenagers were responsible and prepared, despite being too young to have that kind of responsibility.

This did not happen again; we became extremely mindful of weather and what-ifs. Life was never boring, and maybe sometimes we had too much excitement, but we also realized our capacity to rise to the occasion when hit with adversity.

Speaking of high school days, the prom is often a prominent occasion in a high schooler's life. Alex and Carly were not particularly social in high school, and neither of them had a formal date to the prom. One eventually went with a blind date, and the other went last minute with a friend.

And then there was Jess. Jess was legitimately asked to not one but two proms. Her first prom was with Eric. Eric had a disability but was quite verbal, and he adored Jess. We decided to go all out for this event and rented a limo, and Jess wore a beautiful black dress. Mitch and I followed the limo in our car with all the equipment. Jessica's aide attended the prom with Jess because it would have been too embarrassing to have her parents there. She was dazzling and had a wonderful time.

The second time Jess went to the prom was with her classmate, Josh, who loves Jess. Josh has tight curly hair, and he would lower his head so Jess could rub his tresses. He still does this when we run into him in the community. Their prom date was a huge success for both Jess and Josh.

As I ruminated over the sibling experience, I came to what I believe is an obvious conclusion that one does not grow up with a sister like Jessica without fear of his or her own future. Carly described her concern of having a child with a disability. She witnessed firsthand the amount of work and dreaded that this could be her life story. Alex and Carly already went through raising Jess with us, and neither wanted to repeat the story in their own life. We have an acquaintance who has a brother with severe disabilities. The family insisted that the siblings be responsible for their brother once the parents no longer were able to care for their son. Our friend and his wife are responsible one-third of the year for their family member and chose to not have children of their own because of this responsibility. Mitch and I think that is a lot to ask of a sibling.

Alex is known for his lack of patience, so it made me giggle when he said, "I would like to say Jess gave me more patience, but I have no patience." True words! He also thought his perspective on disability was skewed because of Jessica and my field of work; it felt to him that disability was more prevalent in the general population than it actually was, because of our immersion in the situation. "High expectations" was another comment from Alex. He thought we had and still have high expectations from him, higher than other families, but he tempered his statement with saying we also give more of ourselves than many parents.

Alex said that "Jess is instant joy" and "she makes you realize that life is not as bad as you think because if Jess can find a way to be happy, why can't you?" He also lamented that this was an unfair assessment of Jess. "It's not fair to expect Jess to always be happy and it feels jarring to me when she is not cheerful. This is unfair to Jess."

Having Jess as a sister did affect Alex and Carly; of course, their childhood was different from most of their friends. But one cannot assume that the net effect was negative. Carly stated that she was mature beyond her years, which led to self-sufficiency in adulthood. Alex feels that he developed more sensitivity to people who are different.

When I asked Carly if her concept of family is different from others, she replied with a beautiful answer: "Sticking it out and doing what it takes"—she is proud of Mitch and me as a couple because we did couple's counseling and whatever it took to stick out the rough times, and she feels that if we did it, then so can they. I am so proud that Carly can look back at the chaos and caring that was her childhood and see the silver lining.

Both Alex and Carly made a point of saying that life was not that different; Alex stated that "Mom and Dad made every effort to make it not different." Carly said that "we did everything like a normal family, we just 'dragged' Jess."

Most of the information I know about struggling with siblings with disabilities was from research, articles, and blogs. Mitch and I marvel that, at least in public, the people we know who have siblings with disabilities grew up to become caring adults and remain close to their sibling and family. Many people that I have met in the special education field have siblings with disabilities and chose to devote their life work to helping others.

If this is the chapter that was supposed to describe the trauma, despair, and life-altering results of growing up with Jess as a sibling, it didn't come out as expected. Alex and Carly did not speak of trauma or despair. Instead, they highlighted the positives of their early life experience. I know this research could be skewed because I did not have a third-party interviewer ask the questions. It was just me having what I believe was an honest conversation with my kids.

One of the most telling answers I received was from Alex was when I asked, "How would you describe Jess today to somebody you just met?" His reply was, "She's my sister." He did not describe her disability, loud noises, wheelchair, or hardships. It was simple: "She's my sister." True words, Alex.

Jessica, Alex, Carly, and our dog Tracey, 1987.

Carly traveling on Jessica's wheelchair with
Alex and Vickie at Disney World, 1992.

Family trip to Disney, 1992.

Carly, Alex, and Jess, 1990s.

Jess and Carly. (1990s)

Mitch with kids in Florida, 1992.

Vickie, Jess, Alex, and Carly at baseball field.

Vickie, Mitch, Jess, Alex, and Carly
at the group home, 2012.

Family at KanJam World Tournament—Mitch was
co-owner of company until they sold in 2018.[24]

Family portrait at Carly and Steve Smith's
wedding. Jessica was a bridesmaid.

---

[24] www.kanjam.com

Jess and Josh attending Williamsville
East High School Prom, 2003.

Jess and Josh attending Williamsville
East High School Prom, 2003.

CHAPTER 18

The Outlaws

As you know, our family started with Mitch and I, and then we added Jess, Alex, and Carly plus various dogs, a cat, a gerbil, and even two newts along the way. We knew that our family would change once Alex and Carly became adults. Jessica's influence would reach beyond her siblings to include her in-laws or, as our cousin Tony fondly refers to this relationship, the outlaws.

What does it feel like to marry a man or woman whose sibling has severe special needs? I didn't know and decided to ask my friend, Ms. Google, because she knows everything. I even asked her cousin, Ms. Google Scholar, because she knows everything plus adds scholarly literature to her search. I was unable to find any useful information.

Next, I contacted my PhD friend at a local university who teaches graduate students about family dynamics when there is a child with a disability, as well as other topics related to individuals with disabilities. I asked her if she knew of pertinent research on this topic. She did not and asked another professor at the University. Still, we found nothing.

When all else failed, I decided to go directly to the source, which in my case was to Joyce and Steve, Alex and Carly's spouses.

I worried that interviewing them might be harder for them than it was for me. Would they really be honest? If it were me answering the questions, would I be honest? I also wondered if I was creating an issue where there weren't any concerns.

During the fall of 2018, Steve and Carly came from Ohio to visit. I opened the conversation with an update on this book and decided to test the waters by asking Steve a single question: How did he feel when he met Jess for the first time? Steve told me that because he was "raised in a very small community, there were very few people with disabilities," and he didn't even recall meeting a Jewish person before Carly. He continued that an introduction to our family had "opened [his] eyes to a new world and that there is a bigger world out there." Steve added that he, like Jessica's siblings, is also "uncomfortable with the restaurant noises."

After this favorable response, I decided that I wanted to know more about how Joyce and Steve viewed our family. They both seemed to take everything in stride as far as

I was able to observe. In the name of research for this book (and curiosity from this mother-in-law), I asked if I could conduct a formal interview with each of them. Joyce and Steve both agreed.

It wasn't easy for me to ask these questions, but I suspect it was even harder for Joyce and Steve to answer them. In fact, neither interview was done face-to-face. Joyce preferred to correspond via email, and Steve and I had an hour-long conversation on the phone. The fine line between telling it like it is versus potentially insulting your mother-in-law is murky, and I understand that this could have been awkward.

I mentioned in a previous chapter that a friend's girl-friend broke off their relationship when she realized that the future sister-in-law had significant disabilities. So I wondered if meeting Jess caused any initial hesitation to continue dating or consider marrying Alex or Carly. I was pleasantly surprised to find that both Joyce and Steve were prepared by Alex and Carly early into the relationship. Unbeknownst to Mitch and me, this was an important topic to reveal at the outset of a serious romance. Carly and Alex didn't talk to us about the importance of letting suitors know, but it was obviously on the forefront of their minds.

I believe the interview questions resonated with Steve and moved him to think about how much he has changed as an adult. Steve elaborated that most of his neighbors shared the same race, religion, and political views. He admitted that while growing up, he encountered minimal diversity. I worried how he felt about marrying Carly because of Jessica, but maybe I should have been wondering what his family was thinking about Steve marrying a nice Jewish girl!

Steve said that he was a product of his environment, and without having prior experience of disability awareness, it was all new to him. He spent one year in Hawaii at University of Hawaii where, along with having too much fun, he also learned to open his mind to other ways of living. Over the years, Steve has been able to see past Jessica's disability and appreciate the woman who laughs, recognizes people, and has a good quality of life.

At the other end of the spectrum, we have Joyce, who chose to be a special education teacher and knew what she was getting into when marrying Alex. Joyce's comment was, "Alex was very upfront about Jessica and her needs from the beginning, and the way he spoke about her let me know the family had a good grasp on how to incorporate Jessica without marginalizing her." Joyce, because that's who she is, was looking at how our family included Jessica into our lives. She wasn't worried about her potential burden; she was more concerned about Jessica's well-being.

Joyce and Alex live close to us, and she relayed a story that happened before they were married. Jessica was taken by ambulance to the hospital when Mitch and I were out of town. Joyce said, "I felt extremely responsible when it was Alex and I [who are] local and we had to do a few hospitals runs. There was one time we couldn't answer any questions and I [also] had to pretend to be Carly. Vickie and I sat down soon after, and I made a medical history note for Jess in my phone." Not in my wildest dreams did I ever expect that Alex's future wife would be asking me for information so she could better advocate for Jess.

Joyce elaborated, with humor, about the visit to the hospital with Jess. As mentioned above, Joyce told the emergency room personnel that she was Alex's sister, Carly. As she and Alex continued to speak with the nurses and doctors, they must have forgotten their little scheme because they were soon cuddling, holding hands, and acting like boyfriend and girlfriend. The nurse was a bit surprised at their behavior since she thought they were siblings. But I guess nothing is too outlandish in an emergency room!

Both Joyce and Steve were not concerned about their role in Jessica's life because they knew that plans were in place for Jessica's care. This is an important note to families when they are considering long-term care for their child with a disability. Sibling quality of life needs to be an important consideration. Knowing Jessica had support and lived in a group home helped ease the potential conflict that could have arisen.

The term *outlaw* conjures up law-breaking individuals, so it is ironic that our family uses this term to describe beloved family. Perhaps we need to add a newer definition to the Urban Dictionary: Outlaw (n.) cherished family member who marries into your family. Not a blood relative but a chosen relative.

My interviews with Joyce and Steve were completely different, but both revealed insights about their unique perspective and perceived role. I appreciated their honesty and willingness to speak freely with me, and I cherish them both as chosen relatives.

Alex, Joyce, and Griffin.

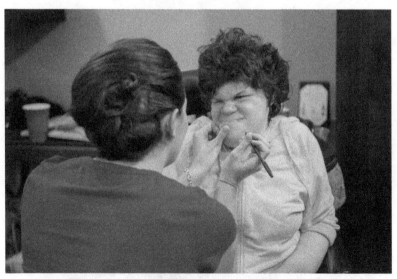

Carly applying lipstick to Jess as they
prep for Carly's wedding.

Carly, Steve, Brady, and Noa.

Family photo, 2018.

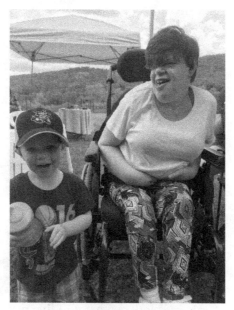

Jessica with nephew Brady.

Carly and Noa visiting Jessica, August 2020. Covid-
19 social distancing and mask wearing protocols
were in place. (Jess would not tolerate a mask)

Jessica, Carly, and Joyce on her wedding day, 2013

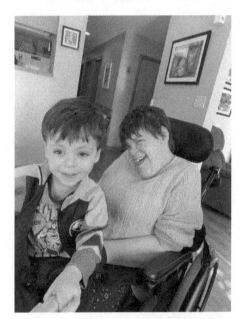

Jessica and nephew Griffin at Jessica house.

Joyce, Alex, and Jess.

Joyce and Alex on their wedding day.

CHAPTER 19

Diagnosis: Does
It Matter?

Some people, if they have the nerve, come up to us and ask a more polite version of "What's wrong with Jess?" by asking, "What is her diagnosis?" The identification of the origin of Jessica's disability was also a puzzle to us. What happened? When Jess was younger and people asked if she had Down syndrome, I would reply, "She has Jessica syndrome." Mitch and I were open to finding more answers as the years passed, but not because we were asking, "Why us?" We had a broader reason to seek solutions.

Throughout my career, I conducted trainings for professionals on "the Parent Perspective when Having a Child with Special Needs." I spoke about our family and then posed the following question to the audience: "Why do you think we kept searching for a diagnosis?" Nobody ever answered this question in the way I was expecting. There were a variety of good responses, including the desire to learn more about the prognosis, to predict future health concerns, or to find other families for support—all true, but not the compelling reason for our continued search.

Jessica's diagnosis sometimes felt like a mystery and could have been an interesting search if it hadn't been affecting our daughter and our family. Jessica had distinctive facial features, and the doctors wanted to check her chromosomes through a blood test.

Mitch and I learned more than we ever wanted to know about chromosomes. Chromosomes dictate who we are and are similar to a blueprint for each person. Chromosomes contain all our DNA. We each have twenty-three pairs of chromosomes equaling a total of forty-six. Each chromosome is composed of a long arm called Q and a short arm called P. When the doctors describe a chromosomal abnormality, they use a number, from 1 to 23, and either the letter p or q to describe the area.

When Jessica was given her first diagnosis, it was called cri du chat (also known as 5P- or five p minus), a deletion in the short arm of the fifth chromosome. This discovery was made by looking at her chromosomes under a light microscope, a technique called a routine karyotypic analysis. After we received the diagnosis, we wanted to learn more about cri du chat, but this was before the days of public internet. Our only resource was the library, which had books with scary photos and outcomes for a young parent. We were essentially alone.

After accepting the diagnosis, Mitch and I took a test that confirmed we were not carriers of cri du chat. This made us comfortable that any future children would not be at risk.

In 1986 a national group of families who have children with cri du chat, Five P Minus Society (https://fivepminus.org), formed, and we quickly joined. Mitch, Jess, and I, along with toddler Alex, traveled to Chicago for one of the meetings where we met the other children with 5P-. We immediately noticed that Jessica did not look like the other kids, yet all the other children had some commonality. It was a bit disheartening and raised the questions if Jessica actually had the same deletion.

In Chicago we met a geneticist who had flown from Florida to participate in the convention. Her specialty was cri du chat, and she agreed that Jessica was dissimilar to the other children and young adults. She asked if she could redraw Jessica's blood and bring it to her lab in Miami for further analysis. We agreed to reinvestigate, knowing this could lead to starting the journey of discovery from scratch.

Several weeks passed, and we were anxious to receive the news. I am not sure if it would have made a difference regarding the services that Jess was receiving, but we believed we needed to know if Jessica's diagnosis was accurate. Did we unknowingly risk having another child when we were looking at the wrong chromosome?

We finally received the results that Jessica did not have cri du chat. No other information was given. The tests revealed no other chromosomal abnormality. We were under the mistaken notion that Jessica had cri du chat for five years, from 1982 to 1987.

We were still left with Jessica's symptoms of severe cognitive and physical delays, the seizures along with the inability to speak or walk, as well as distinguishing facial traits. There was probably a reason for her cognitive and motor delays, but science had not caught up with Jess, so we continued to wait. This was not active waiting; in fact, after a while we went back to our own classification of Jessica syndrome. Our second formal diagnosis came as an offhanded comment made by a physician.

Jess was growing, and by the time she was a teenager, her physical therapist suggested a visit to a physiatrist, a doctor who specializes in rehabilitation and physical medicine.[25] Physiatrists treat a variety of medical conditions that affect the brain, spinal cord, nerves, bones, joints, ligaments, muscles, and tendons. They also help treat pain. This was the first of many annual appointments.

The first day we visited Jessica's physiatrist, he casually explained to me that individuals with cerebral palsy "blah blah blah." That is all I heard after he said cerebral palsy (CP). Jess was an adolescent and not one professional had used this term to describe her. I suspect the doctor thought that this wasn't new information to me, or he wouldn't have

---

[25] For more information about physiatry go to https://www.aapmr.org/about-physiatry/about-physical-medicine-rehabilitation/what-is-physiatry#:~:targetText=Physical%20Medicine%20and%20Rehabilitation%20(PM%26R,ligaments%2C%20muscles%2C%20and%20tendons.&targetText=Diagnose%20and%20treat%20pain%20as,injury%2C%20illness%2C%20or%20disabling%20condition.

casually used the term. It's surprising that CP didn't occur to us prior to that visit. Jess does have many characteristics of an individual with CP such as her spastic (tight) muscle tone, her lack of balance and motor coordination, and her difficulty chewing. It's not that anything changed; Jess and her care remained the same because we were treating unique symptoms, not her diagnosis. It was just another classification on the list of random disorders that describe Jess to medical and clinical professionals. CP explained many of her symptoms, but we still we weren't sure that CP was the correct diagnosis.

Jess did not have a traumatic birth, which is sometimes the cause of CP. My case of chicken pox was scary and distressing, but the actual delivery went relatively smoothly once we were settled at Buffalo Children's Hospital. Something was still missing from this puzzle. Why did she have cerebral palsy?

When Jess was twenty years old, our neighbor, Dr. Laurie Sadler, who is a geneticist at John Oishei Children's Hospital in Buffalo, told us about a new genetic diagnostic test called subtelomeric FISH study (Fluorescence in situ hybridization (FISH),[26] and asked if we wanted to test Jessica. For those of you who are interested in more detail on a FISH study procedure, which in the case of subtelomeric FISH, looks at telomeres (the end portions of the chromosome), see the link below. My knowledge of the procedure ends at the name FISH.

---

[26] For more information about the FISH procedure, see https://www.genome. gov/about-genomics/fact-sheets/Fluorescence-In-Situ-Hybridization.

We immediately said yes to further analysis because we wanted to know if we could identify a different chromosomal abnormality in Jess. The test required a blood sample, similar to Jessica's previous chromosome studies; however, the new procedure was able to identify submicroscopic deletions.

I don't recall how long we waited for the results. It was not like waiting for amniocentesis results. Jessica was here, we knew her thoroughly, and the information from her genetic study would only give us more detail. Jessica was one of the first patients in Buffalo to have this test, and she was the first patient locally who received a positive result, meaning we finally had an answer.

Jessica's chromosomal disorder was now called 1q-43-44 syndrome. Material was missing from the long arm of her number 1 chromosome. When scientists look at chromosomes under the microscope, they stain them so they can see the unique pattern of light and dark bands for each chromosome. This is how they determine which piece or pieces of a chromosome are missing. Think of a chromosome as having stripes of bands around its body; each stripe has a number. The submicroscopic material missing from Jessica's chromosome is in the location of the 43-44 band. This deletion was not visible in previous tests. In fact, Jessica's submicroscopic deletion 1q-43-44 was not detectable until she was twenty years old because the technology was not available until then.

The results still baffle me because I wondered how such a small deletion, smaller than is visible by a typical microscope, could have such a huge impact. The only explanation I have received is that the first chromosome is extremely important, and any missing material can have an enormous effect.

One day, many years later, I was on Facebook and typed in 1q-43-44 in the search box. To my delight, I found a private group of families across the world with a similar diagnosis. This group has been one highlight of finding out Jessica's accurate deletion. I virtually met other families with similar findings.

I immediately joined the group and quickly realized that Jess and I are the oldest members of this group. My theory of why we are the elder members is that many families who have children who are over twenty years of age are not still actively pursuing a diagnosis or don't have the good fortune of having a geneticist living in their neighborhood. My second hypothesis is that even if parents in their fifties are searching for answers about their child's deletion, once they get the results, it is unlikely that they will search for Facebook groups for children with a similar diagnosis. I like these theories better than the thought that there aren't many folks with 1q-43-44 who are still around by the time they are thirty.

We have known Jessica's correct chromosome deletion for seventeen years. The revelation did not change therapies or even medical care, but it gave a name and identity to the various symptoms and beauty that describe Jessica.

Why did we keep searching? What was the answer I gave in all those training sessions? We kept searching because Mitch and I needed to know if Jessica had a hereditary diagnosis. Were either Mitch or I potential carriers? If this proved to be true, then Alex and Carly were at risk of having a child with a similar finding. It's like passing down blue eyes or brown hair, but in our case, we could be passing down a similar fate to their children, our grandchildren.

Mitch and I were tested to see if we were carriers, and fortunately, we were not. Finding this out helped Carly and Alex and their spouses know that they were no more at risk than any other person in the general population. In our case, diagnosis does matter—not because it changed any of our therapies or treatments for Jessica, but because it provided peace of mind for the future of our family.

Celebrating Rare Diagnosis Day—outreach
campaign generated by our private Facebook group.

12/05/2011 13:14   URMC ARRAYCGH LAB   PAGE 02/04

URMC LABS
Strong Memorial Hospital, 601 Elmwood Ave, Rochester, NY 14642
Highland Hospital, 1000 South Ave, Rochester, NY 14620
Ridgeland Road Labs, 77 Ridgeland Rd, Rochester, NY 14623

URMC LABS

Order #: 95287069   FINAL RESULT

Subject information

Subject ID:	
Pedigree:	
Last name:	Rubin First name: Jessica
DOB:	
Sex:	Female
Features:	Short stature; Fine motor delay; Gross motor delay; Speech delay; Mental retardation; Seizures; Dysmorphic facial features; Microcephaly; Congenital hip dislocation
Karyotype:	FISH = ish del(1)(q44)(D1S3739-), performed at Baylor 5/7/1998
Other:	
Consultant:	Women & Children's Hospital of Buffalo
Ordering Clinician:	Dr. Laurie Sadler

ISCN Nomenclature

arr 1q43q44(241,337,300x2, 241,410,546-249,212,639x1)

Findings = Positive

Karyotype View

[karyotype chromosome image]

95287069: Jessica Rubin - 267391659 d - Karyotype Chart (Rejoined) 12/15/2011

Printed: 12/5/2011 11:35:56 AM   Page 1 of 3

Order #: _____ D: Rubin, Jessica

Jessica's official diagnosis.

CHAPTER 20

You Changed My Life

Having Jess changed the course of my life. She changed Mitch's life, and she paved the road for the lives of her siblings.

Jessica's diagnosis moved me from a somewhat spoiled girl from Long Island, whose priorities were cool clothes and designer purses, to a regionally known champion for families of children with special needs—who still loves a fancy purse. This did not happen overnight.

I initially enrolled in the master's program for exceptional education to become a better advocate for Jess, but what happened was much bigger than our little story.

When I was hired as a parent educator at the Early Childhood Direction Center, my future boss saw more potential in me than I saw in myself. I still knew nothing about the state and federal regulations for individuals with disabilities, but I knew how to study and research—and I had twenty years of experience raising Jessica.

Fast-forward eighteen years later to June 2017 at the time of my retirement party. I retired as the director of the West New York Early Childhood Direction Center, one of fourteen centers across New York State. To this day, I still come across families who tell me that I taught them skills that changed how they advocated for their children. I believe I shared the belief of hope with other families and gave guidance about advocating for their child "with honey instead of vinegar."

The Honorable Ruth Bader Ginsburg advises, "Fight for the things that you care about, but do it in a way that will lead others to join you." Championing for Jess and others in our community was never about going to war. Negotiation, planning, education, and conversation are far more influential than screaming and anger. Over the years I spoke with families who were ready to call a lawyer before they even met their district representatives. The goal is to lead others down your path, which is not easy, especially in the heat of the moment. Another quote from the Notorious RBG is, "I'm a very strong believer in listening and learning from others." Listening is a key component to successful advocacy. Advocating for better outcomes for others instills hope that circumstances will improve.

While working in the hospital, I attended a meeting about talking with parents. One of the key components of the conversation centered around the concept of hope.

Families need hope from those surrounding them. Medical professionals, teachers, clinicians, coordinators of service, family members, and friends have a powerful tool when it comes to supporting the family of children with special needs. Help that family choose to hope, for without hope, you have despair.

Jessica has achieved goals we never thought possible. She learned how to say "Mama" and "Hi, Mama" when she was eighteen. One day she looked at me and repeated, "Ma-ma-ma-ma-ma." She says this often, but not to call me from across the room. Instead, Jess sometimes looks me in the eye and repeats her mantra, and her intensity lets me know that she is talking directly to me. We hoped that Jess would be able to speak.

She hums about thirty-five tunes perfectly, from the "Jeopardy!" theme to a Hebrew prayer tune to "Twinkle, Twinkle, Little Star." She has picked up many of these songs on her own. We hoped that Jess would be able to find joy in music.

She also mastered one useful sign. Jess puts a flat hand over her mouth when she wants to communicate anything from "yes" to "I want a hug/kiss" to "I want chocolate." We have tried to get her to differentiate these signs, but so far, she chooses to use this one for many meanings. As I said previously, one must know Jess's code. We hoped Jess would be able to communicate.

When Jess lived at home, she refused to move her wheelchair independently. Was she being a princess? Did she know that I would eventually push her chair, so why should she bother? Jess is no longer immobile; she can navigate a three-point turn with her wheelchair as if she is driving a race car. She gets where she wants to go. We hoped that Jess would be more independent with her chair.

Jessica owns an iPad and consistently selects "yes" or "no" when asked a question—only if she's interested. This can be frustrating, but I understand this is Jessica's way of having some control in her life. We hoped that Jess would have more control in her life.

Jessica also owns an iPhone. Our beloved friend and former case manager, Kasey, suggested an iPhone so that Jess could independently listen to her music. I questioned this purchase because Jessica tends to throw items to the floor. The iPhone, however, was a game changer in terms of Jessica independently seeking recreation. Jess sits in her chair, iPhone to ear (like a mini boombox) and listens to her tunes with a broad smile. After a long period, she may toss her phone, but a super-strong phone case has solved that problem. We hoped that Jess would be able to independently enjoy her phone and use it successfully.

During the day, Jessica is in a Day Habilitation program. Her teacher recently told me that Jessica's communication has increased since they added a picture board to the wall. Jess will independently move her wheelchair to the board and point to the piano. A note from Jessica's teacher, Ashley, said, "We started Jessica's communication wall and she has gotten to the point that she will actually wheel herself over, point to the piano, and sign 'please.'" We hoped that others, nonfamily members, would see Jessica's potential and abilities.

Raising Jess is our story of hope. And what is hope? We believe hope can be found in family, it can be found in friends, and it can be found in groups of people with similar experiences. Hope is all around if you are looking for it.

Jessica has friends, family, nephews, and a niece. She is an integral part of our family and her community. Our hope for a future where Jess is happy and able to participate has come true.

Jessica in a specialized racing wheelchair.
She and Vickie completed a community
race with the group Buffalo Racin.[27]

---

[27] http://www.buffaloracin.org/

Certificate celebrating 15 years at ARC of
Erie Day Habilitation Program, 2019.[28]

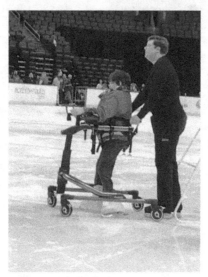

Jessica participating in SABAH skating program.[29]

---

[28] https://www.arceriecounty.org/
[29] https://sabahinc.org/

Jessica at the piano with Jenna (music therapist
at Buffalo Hearing and Speech Center)[30]

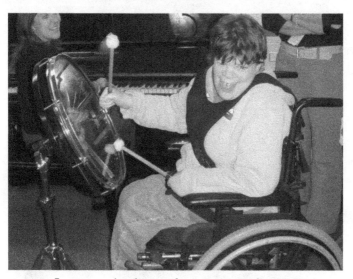

Jessica at the drums during music therapy.

---

[30] https://askbhsc.org/music-therapy-services-for-children

EPILOGUE

I started writing this book in 2017 before coronavirus or COVID-19 were everyday vernacular.

Mitch and I drove to Key Largo in Southern Florida at the end of February 2020. We planned to stay in a rented home for one month. The radio was tuned to the news as we traveled deep into the southern states. Most of the media focused on the story of a virus that had traveled from China and landed in Washington State, devastating nursing homes.

In the summer of 2020, we planned to travel across the country. It was a trip we spoke of for forty years, and we were eagerly planning to drive to all the national parks. The news raised fears about going far west. Perhaps we would skip Washington State and other western territories. Little did we know.

Our first week in Florida coincided with increased news coverage and anxiety. I went to the local store to buy hand sanitizer and found that they were sold out. This was concerning and surprising to me at the time. I eventually found hand sanitizer at a dollar store. It was hidden in an aisle presumably unknown to the store clerk as she had told me they were also sold out.

Each evening, the news of the spread of coronavirus was blaring in our rental vacation home. There was no respite. We did not realize that this was only the beginning of what would become a pandemic of unprecedented proportions in our lifetime.

Thoughts of Jessica's safety were few at first because the virus was way out in the west. Quickly, the virus started spreading and New York City was hit aggressively. I received a call from a friend at People Inc. who cautioned that Jessica may be better off living at our home if the trajectory of the virus continued its path. We received this call on March 16, 2020.

On March 17, we woke up and said we needed to escape ASAP. Okay, escape is my word. Mitch just agreed to drive home. Why leave the Keys? We were able to sit outside, walk in the sun, and sit on a boat. And, at that time, there weren't any diagnosed cases of coronavirus in Monroe County, Florida.

Our sense of family brought us back even though New York State was one of the most affected states. We drove twenty-eight hours straight through to get home. We used an apocalyptic toilet (a large bucket) so as not to go in public bathrooms. This is something that I never thought I would be able to do, but nothing was the same anymore—new rules for a new time. We shopped for food in West Virginia since they had the least amount of COVID-19 cases and continued our drive back to New York State.

We planned to bring Jess home if needed, and we wanted to be available if the time arose for Jess to relocate. Caring for Jess after thirteen years her of living in a group home would not be easy. Our house did not have the specialized equipment, and our sixty-year-old backs were no longer able to do the lifting required to care for Jess. Additionally, our daughter and son-in-law and our two grandchildren, ages four and six months, were moving into our home on April 1.

Day care centers were closing, and Mitch and I were planning on providing childcare five days a week for our grandchildren. Would we be able to provide the additional daily care that Jess needed?

I received a call from Kelly, Jessica's house manager. Kelly said she was required to ask if we would be able to care for Jess at home if needed. We immediately said yes because the alternative could have been that Jess would be placed in another location.

Kelly also told us to calm down because, at this point, she had everything under control. Staff was asked to limit their exposure when they were not working, take on extra hours, and dedicate themselves to the care of the four ladies who ultimately remained at the house. As time wore on and the virus ravaged New York City and other major areas, Kelly, supported by People Inc., managed to keep our daughter and her housemates safe. Most of the women in Jessica's house are vulnerable, and every day we still woke up, thinking, "Is this the day that someone will be exposed?"

Mitch and I were no longer able to visit Jess.

How do we explain to Jess that we are unable to visit her, to give her a hug and kisses? That we cannot hold her hand or look at videos and photos on my phone together? That we cannot share a chocolate decadent cake or go outside for a walk, that her siblings, nephew, and niece or her friends, Sheryl, and Ellen can't visit?

Jessica's group home is two miles from our house, but she may as well be two hundred miles away since families are not allowed to enter her home, and she is not permitted to exit. We are thankful to her house manager, Kelly, and staff who are strictly keeping these rules.

So we FaceTimed. Jessica's superpower is connecting with those she loves, and it was no surprise that she was able to embrace and engage in FaceTiming. She does not appear sad that we are not there in person. Her smile and joy emanate through the phone at seeing our faces and hearing our voices.

One day, Mitch and I were FaceTiming with Jessica and decided we would try to have a conversation with music. Mitch was the videographer with his phone while I started humming a familiar Jewish prayer to Jessica. (See Facebook page RaisingJessStory for the actual video https://www.facebook.com/RaisingJessStory/.)

Jess looked at me, rubbed her nose, and immediately hummed the prayer back to me! We were talking, we were singing, we were communicating, and we were speaking the language of love and music.

We have sung with Jess in the past and she usually takes several minutes to sing the song back to us, but this time, the pause in between my singing and her reply was conversational—immediate.

It took fifty-four days until we were able to visit Jessica in person at a distance. I was not sure how this was going to play out. Jess enjoyed our FaceTime visits, but I was concerned that she would not understand why we were unable to touch her even though we were visibly in front of her. Mitch insisted that we needed to visually look at Jess, and he wanted Jess to know that we were here, not just on her iPad or iPhone.

I desperately wanted to see Jess, but was concerned that it might frustrate her more than comfort. Would Jess understand that we were unable to give a hug or hold her hand? Were we doing more harm than good? It was a risk we needed to take because there was no telling when we would be able to embrace Jessica without fear of unknowingly spreading COVID-19.

We drove up the driveway and saw Jess and her housemates waiting on the porch. Three dedicated staff were also waiting to say hello for the first time since February 26th.

Mitch and I got out of the car and walked on the grass while Jess remained on her porch. We were a solid twenty feet away, but we were there in person.

Jessica's reaction was one we were hoping for: she clapped her hands and screamed with glee. Jess did not try to move her chair, nor did she seem frustrated by the distance between us. She was thrilled to see us, which gave all of us a lift during this dark time.

Mitch and I hummed a few tunes, and Jess replied with the second verse: our special communication. We brought our therapy dog, Daniel, who also howled a few tunes and made the ladies and staff smile and laugh.

Kelly and the devoted staff have overwhelmed us with their commitment, love, and dedication to keep our daughter as safe as possible. Mitch and I know that Jess is just one exposure away from devastation. We are forever grateful for the care she is receiving and continue to pray, wish, and hope that her safety continues.

We have all lost a lot of control of our normal day-to-day lives during the pandemic. Slowly, we are trying to regain our footing and although things may be different, that does not mean we will be worse off. I hope the lessons learned from this scary and unprecedented experience will lead us to a better tomorrow. I look forward to holding Jessica's hands, receiving huge hugs, and I will even tolerate Jess playfully pulling my messy, out-of-control hair!

Jess and Vickie
Photo by Michelle Godfrey Photo

POSTSCRIPT

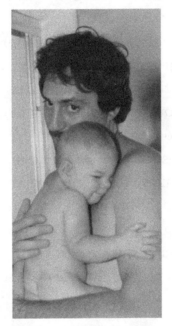

Jessica and Mitch, 1982.

A Letter to Mitch

Dear Mitch,

Our early years were hard on both of us, and in this book, you sometimes get the bad rap. We were only twenty-four years old and had so much responsibility on our shoulders. This story is from my perspective, and I am sure that you have a book in you that would give a different perspective on my behavior. Please don't write it!

You are sometimes called Mitzvah Man, and I believe that a lot of who I became is not only because of Jess; you played a huge role in recreating my value system.

Over the years, you have mentored numerous people who needed assistance. You are a genuinely giving person who wants to help and not for the congratulations, it's who you are—behind the scenes doing the right thing.

I describe you in this book as a non-rule follower and someone who likes to take the lead, but what I don't describe enough is the loving, giving man you are. When I write in the acknowledgements that you experienced the same challenges as me but got so little credit for doing anything, it's true.

I wouldn't want anyone else by my side during this journey, and I feel blessed that we chose each other.

Love,
Vickie

Mitch and Jess dancing at a pub on her 21st birthday.

Jess and Mitch.
Photo by Michelle Godfrey Photo

ACKNOWLEDGMENTS

My sincere thanks—

To Mitch, who lived through the same journey but got so little credit for his role raising Jessica. Mitch was my very first editor and read and listened to ALL THE early drafts. For encouraging me to keep going and believing in me. Thank you so much. I love you!

To Jessica, you have inspired me to become a better person. Your charm, song, and smile bring joy to all who meet you. You are my first child and taught me how to mother and love in ways I never knew possible.

To Alex and Joyce, who encouraged me continue to write my book and went as far as buying me an old-school thesaurus, dictionary, and other tools to start the process. And to Alex, one of my key editors, because I knew if he was agreeable to the copy, then I was on the right track.

To Carly and Steve, who listened to my chapters and gave awesome feedback and interviews. And to Carly for giving an honest opinion about the drafts.

To my late mother, who nagged (motivated) by saying, "You need to write a book!" I hope that you know how thankful I am for giving me the confidence to attempt this project.

To Dad, who gave me details from the back of his brain where he says he keeps countless facts and random information and for his honesty when providing details for this manuscript. Most importantly, for reading each chapter to Mom as they were completed.

To Marty, my father-in-law, for always eliciting a beautiful smile and gleeful joy from Jess. And to his wife Norma, for always accepting, loving, and appreciating our family. It means a lot.

To our siblings and their families, who were not mentioned in the book but are a huge presence and support in our life. Keith and Cathy Schlanger and Scott and Evie Rubin and all the cousins treat Jess with love and kindness and, because they live out of state, have not been part of our day-to-day existence; nevertheless, they have been part of our village, and for that we are grateful. Special shout-out to my brother-in-law Scott Rubin, former Editor-in-Chief of National Lampoon, for guidance and advice.

To Sheryl, Ellen, and Barbara and their families, who continue to give our family support, hope, and unconditional love and friendship.

To Rick and Susan Zurak, who share our family holidays and show Jess love and kindness. We know you have our backs and thank you for your never-ending support.

To Beth, Phyllis, and Ruth, who encouraged me throughout the entire book-writing process and have been my listeners for over thirty years!

To Sue Goldman, who captured Jessica and me in the beautiful book cover photo. Sue and I have been friends since 4th grade when it was cool to be older than your friends! Yes, I am one year older! Sue created a world of beauty with her photography, and I am in awe of her talent and blessed with her friendship. www.SusanGoldmanPhotography.com

To Kelly Special, who is truly *special* and makes it possible for Mitch and me to relax when we are not with Jessica. She runs Jessica's home with skill, love, expertise, and kindness. We know that Jessica is in good hands with Kelly as her home manager.

To all the fantastic staff who help Jessica with skill, enthusiasm, and love each and every day. A few of Jessica's champions are Jill, Eric, Antione, Areyania, Michelle, and Dwight.

To the women in Jessica's home and their families, who comprise our second family by sharing the love of our daughters and keeping a parental eye on all the women. To Cathy and Larry Skerker, who have become our family by choice as we share joy, sadness, support, advocacy, and love for our daughters in the group home, where Jessica and their daughter Lizzy both live. Group home life does not run well in isolation, and the families have transformed this house from a standard residential site to a treasured family home.

To the late Jill Popkin, Jessica's housemate and friend who passed in 2018. Jill and her family became our family, and we will miss her lovely smiles, sense of humor, warm hugs, and spirited personality.

To the late Maury and Dorothy Connock and to their family, who were our next-door neighbors for the first four years of Jessica's life. They embraced Jessica as their own, and they were one of the reasons that we were able to survive the first few years. Their son Craig, who is our friend, goes monthly to Jessica's house to cut her hair. He snips, and she squirms; his patience and skill are second to none.

To Kasey Gorman, who started as Jessica's Medicaid Service Coordinator and became a treasured family friend. Kasey was an advocate for Jess and our family, and she walked the extra mile to ensure Jessica's safety. Kasey is no longer Jessica's. service coordinator in theory, but she is still my go-to. I trust Kasey completely to help make service decisions about Jess.

To Janet Gunner for her vision and knowledge that Jessica's home could be a possibility. Her leadership, guidance, and dedication to our daughter's home and the community is unparalleled. And to the wonderful volunteers from Temple Beth Tzedek and Jewish Federation of Buffalo (Yad B Yad), who volunteer monthly at Jessica and her housemates' home to provide programming.

To Congregation Shir Shalom (formerly Temple Sinai), Cantor Arlene Frank and Rabbi Alex Lazarus-Klein for always including Jessica and our family. To Rabbi Alex for embracing Jessica's version of praying through music.

To People Incorporated for making sure that the women are healthy and safe. We selected People Inc. to build and oversee Jessica's home because we were (and still are) confident in their leadership, knowledge, expertise, fairness, and humanity of administrators.

To all my coworkers at ECDC—Stacie, Ruth, Tracey, and Lauren who were tolerant of the time I had to miss work when Jessica was sick and the many appointments that I needed to attend, who were supportive of Jessica and our family and became not only coworkers but friends.

To the staff of Parent Network of Western New York, who provided, and still provide, guidance and advocacy assistance and to their executive director, Sue Barlow, who became a colleague, advocate, and most importantly, a friend.

To 1Q4 Deletions-Family Support who opened my eyes to other families with the same or similar diagnosis. This small but mighty international group stands by each other as we share joy, sorrow, frustration, milestones, and pride. They have made a difference in our life.

To Dr. Laurie Sadler, who solved our mystery and used her editing and medical expertise to make sure that I got the genetic details correct.

To Lois Swagerty, my editor, who was able to fix all my errors while keeping the narrative true to my voice, for answering all the questions from this first-time book writer and providing me with encouraging and valuable feedback.

To Chuck Shank, Literary Development agent and Nicole Refer, Publication coordinator for Page Publishing, Inc. for guiding this "newbie" through a daunting process. For answering my questions and there were many! And for helping make my dream come true.

To all our family and friends not mentioned specifically in this book, but always appreciated for all the support you have given us so that we can live a story of hope.

Rick and Susan Zurak with Vickie
and Mitch at Bill's Stadium.

Top left: Vickie and Ruth, Top Right: Beth
and Vickie, Bottom: Phyllis and Vickie.

Dwight and Jess.

Eric, former staff, and Jess at her house.

Antione and Jessica.

Jill, former house manager, and Jessica.

Kelly, current house manager, and Jessica.

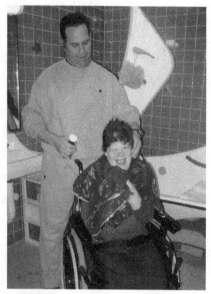

Craig cutting Jessica's hair in her home.

Maury and Dorothy Connock our next-
door neighbors from 1982–1986.

Jess, Alex, Carly, and first cousins
Corey and Jared Schlanger.

Keith and Cathy with Brady and Griffin, 2018

Miles, Risa, and Zane Rubin,
Jessica's first cousins. (2006).

Mitch's brother Scott and our sister-in-law
Evie along with the Rubin first cousins.

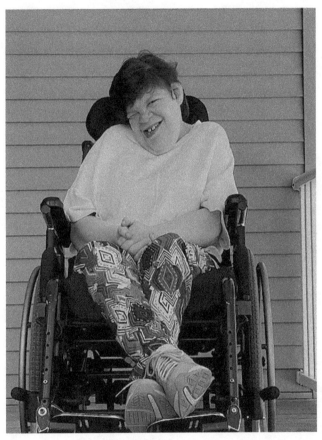

Jessica Rubin, 2020.

ABOUT THE AUTHOR

Photo by Michelle Godfrey Photo

Vickie Rubin, M.S. Ed. was born in Queens, New York in 1957 and raised in suburban Westbury, Long Island. She received her Bachelor's with honors in Elementary Education and Early Childhood Education from the University of Miami in 1979.

Vickie earned her Master's in Exceptional Education at Buffalo State College (2001) where she was awarded The President's Medal for Outstanding Graduate Student at Buffalo State and the Bernard Yormak Award for Outstanding Graduate Student in Exceptional Education.

As the long standing Manager of Early Childhood Direction Center (ECDC) for Oishei Children's Hospital, Kaleida Health/ Project Director of the New York State Education Department ECDC program, Vickie was a frequent guest speaker at colleges and universities throughout New York State. She continued to share her knowledge serving as an adjunct teacher in the Exceptional Education Department at Buffalo State College.

Vickie and her family received the Community Recognition Award for their exceptional contributions to the community of children with special needs and their families. The award was presented by The Children's Guild Foundation, Buffalo, New York.

Vickie is a frequent contributor to the Buffalo News having numerous stories published in the multiple Pulitzer prize winning journal.

She has a popular blog, Vickie's Views (https://vickierubin.com/) where she posts heartwarming and inspiring stories of everyday life.

Vickie and her husband Mitch have been married for forty-one years and they are the parents of three adult/children. They lovingly have added their daughter-in-law and son-in-law into their family. Vickie and Mitch are the proud Nana and Papa of two grandsons and one granddaughter. They also have two dogs, Gus (Vizsla) and Daniel (Italian Greyhound). Vickie is thankful that you spent some time learning about her family and hopes that this book brought you some inspiration, joy, and hope.